LOVE and SEX
in plain language

Also by the Author

ERIC W. JOHNSON

LOVE and SEX
in plain language

Fourth Revised Edition

1817

HARPER & ROW, PUBLISHERS, New York
Cambridge, Philadelphia, San Francisco, London, Mexico City,
São Paulo, Singapore, Sydney

Grateful acknowledgment is made for permission to reprint:

The illustration on page 45 from *The Individual, Sex, and Society*, edited by Carlfred Broderick and Jessie Bernard, 1969. Reprinted by permission of The Johns Hopkins University Press.

Excerpt on pages 109–110 from *Reaching Your Teenager* by Elizabeth C. Winship. Copyright © 1983 by Elizabeth C. Winship. Reprinted by permission of Houghton Mifflin Co.

Designed by Ruth Bornschlegel

Illustrations by Russ Hoover except pages 10 and 22 by Gary Tong and pages 8 and 17 by Russ Hoover and Gary Tong.

Library of Congress Cataloging in Publication Data

Johnson, Eric W.
  Love and sex in plain language.

  Includes index.
  Summary: Describes development of sexual characteristics in boys and girls; explains the physiology of intercourse, pregnancy, and birth; and discusses homosexuality, masturbation, contraception, and VD.
  1. Sex instruction for youth. [1. Sex instruction for youth] I. Title.
HQ35.J56 1985   613.9′5   84-48170
ISBN 0-06-015418-7

86 87 88 10 9 8 7 6 5 4 3 2

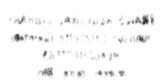

Contents

Foreword

In the area of love and sex, the old adage "What you don't know won't hurt you" doesn't work. What you don't know may very well hurt you—and those around you. In *Love and Sex in Plain Language*, Eric Johnson provides knowledge of anatomy, sexual physiology, ways of thinking, varied intimacies, and methods for avoiding distress, disease, and unwanted pregnancies.

This book serves as a valuable means for developing responsible decision-making, for preventing trouble, and for aying the groundwork for the healthy enjoyment of sexuality. It encourages the rightly curious young to engage in give-and-take discussions with their parents and teachers as well as with one another. With information such as this, ignorance can no longer serve as an excuse for behavior that may result in disaster or for fears that may take much of the joy out of living and loving.

During my professional and personal life, I have spent many hours with young and older people discussing their feelings, their attitudes, their questions and hopes and fears. I have tried to encourage them to communicate with each other about their values and expectations and the effect these have on their behavior and relationships in the loving side of life. I have long since learned how different from one another people are and how vital it is to understand and respect their differences, which are based both on the genes with which each of us begins life and on the environment within which each of us develops.

I believe *Love and Sex in Plain Language* respects these differences, and especially the differences in attitudes, experience, and conviction that each reader may have. The book can play an important part in the growth of strength, happiness, and responsible action for people of all ages who read and discuss the clear and practical information it presents with such human warmth and understanding.

EMILY H. MUDD, PH.D.

*Professor Emeritus of Family Study in Psychiatry
and Consultant in Behavioral Studies,
Department of Obstetrics and Gynecology,
University of Pennsylvania School of Medicine
Past President of the American Association of
Marriage and Family Counselors*

Preface

This book is written for boys and girls, and for older people as well. The writing is easy enough for most ten-year-olds to understand; the information and ideas presented will be useful to many college students. I suggest that when boys and girls show interest in the subject of sex, you let them have the book, but do not push it on them. And first read it yourself. Then you will have a common basis for discussion.

The book can also be used as a text for a unit in sex education in middle school, junior high school, or in some cases, high school. Although it is written in "plain language," it does not talk down to anyone.

Love and Sex in Plain Language is based on some common assumptions. I assume that sex is a part of life—only a part, but a very important, healthy, and natural part. I assume that the power of sex, for good and for evil, for pleasure and for hurt, is so great that we must make every effort to see that it is used responsibly. I assume that to act responsibly people need all the relevant knowledge that they can understand. Mistakes are made not because of too much knowledge, but because of too little, or because of bits of knowledge used out of perspective.

The facts can be understood best in a framework of values: caring, responsibility, self-control, the family, faithfulness, honesty, love, respect of self and others, and the goodness of life. I hope this book strengthens these values.

Some books on sex written for young people do not have

an index, I suppose because the writers fear that the readers will turn to the hottest spots and then read no further. This book has a complete index, and I would consider it entirely natural if readers turn first to the topics that interest them most. If they find that these topics are treated frankly, fully, but concisely, then probably they will read the book all the way through. But no one should be forced to read more than he or she wants to read.

Also, if people read the entire book, it should be easy for them to find again quickly those parts they need to reread. Few people will be able to absorb all there is in the book during a single reading.

The book is plain, open, and frank. I hope that reading it will make your children and your students more ready to ask questions of you and of each other. If they ask you, I suggest that you answer them as plainly, openly, and frankly as you can. If they do not, don't be too disappointed. A free family dialogue on sexual matters is surprisingly rare. Most boys and girls, especially after they reach adolescence, just don't seem to want such openness, or if they do want it, to be able to put themselves in a situation to have it. This is why sex education in schools can be important as a supplement to the primary sex education given by parents.

I first wrote this book in 1965. The present edition represents the fourth time I have revised it. Why, if the basic human geography stays the same, does a book on love and sex need to be revised so often? There are three reasons. First, scientists constantly learn more about the physical facts of sexuality and how they relate to our lives. Second, attitudes toward human sexuality—even toward the basic physical facts—change, and these new attitudes must be discussed. And third, the society in which we live our sexual lives changes, and these changes must be dealt with. No one ever finishes his or her sex education, neither the writers of books nor their readers. If you look back on your own sex education—or lack of it—you will see the truth of this.

Everyone wants to know "everything" about sex. Making that possible for your children will help bring you closer in trust and love.

I welcome opinions from parents, teachers, students, and teenagers on what they find of value in this book and also on how I might improve it. Write to me in care of Harper & Row, 10 East 53rd Street, NY, NY 10022.

During my work on the four editions of this book, I have been unusually fortunate to have the facts checked and points of view critically analyzed by some of the country's outstanding teachers, doctors, and specialists in obstetrics and gynecology, psychology, psychiatry, sex education, sexology, family planning, and family relations. I am most grateful to these people for the many hours of assistance they have given. Their names are listed near the end of this book, on pages 141–144.

Eric W. Johnson

CHAPTER ONE

Why talk plainly about love and sex?

After school one day I was talking with a boy I was teaching in English class. He had read a book I had written about junior high school, and he asked, "Mr. Johnson, are you ever going to write another book?"

I told him I planned to write one about sex and that it would be primarily for people his age. "I'm having a hard time deciding how much to put into it," I told him. "Maybe you can help me. What do you think people your age want to know about sex?"

"Everything!" he replied at once and with a sure smile.

And every student I have talked with since then has given almost the same reply. So I decided that in this book I would try to tell everything, and to tell it in plain language.

But before we get down to the detailed facts of sex and love, you should understand a few general ideas, which will help you to understand the facts better.

Everyone of almost any age is interested in sex, in the differences between boys and girls and men and women, in lovemaking, in what starts babies, and in how they develop and are born. People are interested in questions about sexual behavior and feelings, about sex outside of the family as well as inside. Your own interest in these things, even though you may find it difficult to admit it to everyone or even to yourself, is perfectly normal. After all, why shouldn't a person want to know all about such an important and universal a thing as sex? Without it the human race would soon disappear. It affects our most important human relationships and can be one of our greatest pleasures.

Yet many parents and other adults are uncomfortable when they try to talk about sex. Perhaps your parents have talked with you about it; perhaps they have not. Perhaps, like many adults, they were brought up to believe that sex is very personal and private—so it is easy to understand why they may hesitate to discuss it with you.

A young girl wrote to me once saying that it was difficult for her to get any information about sex from her parents because she was too embarrassed to start asking questions. She told me that when she finally did get the courage to ask one, her father said, "See your mother," and her mother said, "I'm busy."

Perhaps after you have read this book you will be able to ask questions and express opinions more easily, and that will make it easier for your parents and teachers to try to answer your questions and to listen to your opinions and give you theirs.

Because people's interest in sex is so natural and so strong, and because people so often don't want to talk about it, many wrong ideas get passed around. You can help others as well as yourself by learning the facts and by correcting any wrong ideas you may hear. If you have unanswered questions, the only intelligent thing to do is to ask them of a mature person you respect and who knows the answers, preferably your mother or father, your teacher, clergyman or -woman or rabbi, or your doctor. And, of course, there are lots of questions about sexual behavior that you may try all your life to answer.

Many people don't like to admit there's anything about sex that they don't know. But surely the best policy is to admit what you don't know and to try to find out about it. Most people will respect you for this.

Sex can be a powerful urge. By the time people reach their middle teens, their interest in sexual activity may be quite strong. However, the strength of this urge varies from person to person and from time to time, and in many people other interests are much stronger.

The important thing for you to know is that sex can be a wonderful expression of love between people and can give great pleasure. But, as with almost anything so powerful, it can also cause much suffering if used thoughtlessly or ignorantly. It can create families and bind them together; it can damage them and break them up. Later chapters will say more about these matters.

CHAPTER TWO

Some values to guide you

By now you may be thinking, "O.K., let's get to the facts."
O.K., in a few pages we shall! First, though, you should be
prepared to make your own decisions about sex, love, and life
as you read this book. You may find it helpful to consider a set
of values to provide some background against which to make
these decisions.

• The first value is the **infinite worth of each individual
person.** This includes yourself and others. Don't forget that
self-respect is the beginning of respect for others and for their
worth.

• The second value is **consideration.** You consider and
care both for your own needs, feelings, worth, and welfare and
also for those of others. To be truly considerate of others, you
must have enough thoughtfulness and imagination to put
yourself in their shoes, to try to understand their situation and
their ways of thinking and feeling.

• The third value is **communication.** It is good to be able
to talk things over with other people. How else can you know
their needs, thoughts, and feelings, and how else can they
consider yours? It is good for people to be able to talk with
each other about their sexual feelings, desires, and fears. (This
book will help you to communicate with your parents, your
friends, your teachers. Often when people have all read the
same book, the way to communication is more easily opened
to them.)

• The fourth value is the **family.** The family is one of the main bases of a healthy society, and for most people, the best way to grow up is as part of a healthy, loving, sharing family. You should consider your sexual actions on the basis of whether they will strengthen and enrich your family, the families of others, and any family you may help to create.

• The fifth value is **responsibility.** If you are a responsible person, before you act you think about what the results of your action will be. You consider the results of these actions not only for yourself but also for others, and not just for today but for the future as well.

• The sixth value is **pleasure and good feelings.** We all know, and have known since we were infants, that our bodies can give us good feelings. For many people—though not all—feelings of bodily pleasure, called sensual feelings, are an important part of a good life, right through old age.

• The seventh value is **control.** Sex is a power. Like any other power, it can be used for good or for bad. You learn to control your sexual power so that you use it for good—the good of yourself and of others.

• The eighth value is that of **information.** Correct information—the facts—is better than ignorance or rumor. Sound information makes it possible for you to act responsibly. Ignorance may get you into trouble.

And now we turn first to several chapters of information.

CHAPTER THREE

The woman's sex organs and how they develop and work

In this chapter I'll tell you about girls and women, and in the one that follows, about boys amd men. It's important for all people to know about both. As you read the explanations, refer to the drawings of a grown woman on the following page and to the more detailed diagram of her **genitals***, or sexual parts.

The **ovaries** are where the egg cells (**ova**) are stored. These two organs are inside the lower part of the **abdomen**, one on either side, and are the shape of a flattened oval, about 1¼ to 2½ inches long. When a female baby is born, her ovaries already contain, in undeveloped form, tens of thousands of egg cells. Four to five hundred of them will mature during her lifetime. But the ovaries are inactive until a girl reaches **puberty.** Then, around the ages of eleven to fourteen—but perhaps earlier, perhaps later—they begin an intricate monthly process called the **menstrual cycle,** which is repeated more or less regularly until a woman reaches the age of forty-five (or possibly younger) to fifty-five. During these thirty to forty years, every twenty-one to thirty-five days, a mature egg (**ovum**) is produced by one or the other ovary. The egg cell is very small; a row of two hundred would be only about an inch long. The ovum bursts through the surface of the ovary and enters the **fallopian tube** just next to it, helped by the movements of the tube's fingerlike fringes, called **fimbria.** This process is called **ovulation.**

*Some words are printed in boldface as, for example, **genitals,** usually the first time they are used. This means, in most cases, that you can find their definitions in the glossary, the word list beginning on page 117.

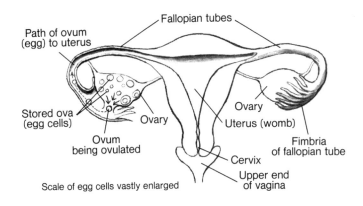

OVULATION   (scale of egg cells vastly enlarged)

After ovulation, the ovum is moved slowly down the fallopian tube toward the **uterus,** also called the **womb.** This organ, located between the ovaries, is pear-shaped and about 3 inches long in a mature female who has not had children. It is muscular and elastic and can grow and stretch to many times this size. The uterus is the organ in which a baby grows until it is ready to be born. Its muscles are quite powerful and help to push the baby out through the **vagina,** or **birth canal,** into the world.

In every menstrual cycle, the uterus prepares for a fertilized egg, an egg which may grow into a baby. It creates a nourishing, soft webbing, like a velvety lining, of tiny, delicate blood vessels, called the **endometrium.** This is a perfect place for the egg to grow in. If an egg is fertilized, it has already started to grow by the time it enters the uterus, about three or four days after it left the ovary.

However, if an egg is not fertilized, it stays alive for only about twelve to twenty-four hours after entering the fallopian tube, and then it breaks up and is absorbed into the body. In this case, the growing place in the uterus is not needed, and the lining, blood, and blood vessels are discarded through the

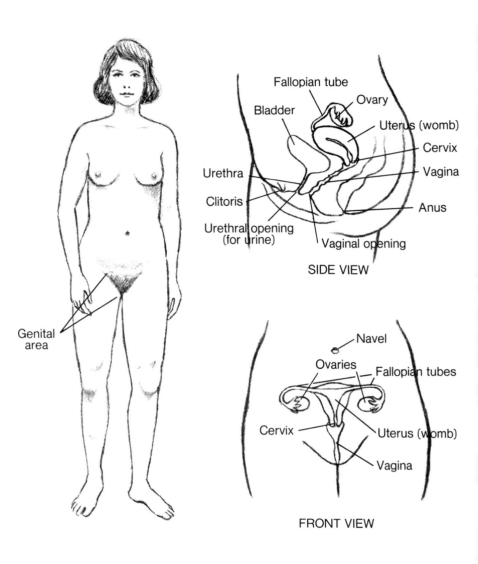

Fallopian tube

Ovary

Bladder

Uterus (womb)

Cervix

Urethra

Vagina

Clitoris

Anus

Urethral opening
(for urine)

Vaginal opening

SIDE VIEW

Genital
area

Navel

Ovaries

Fallopian tubes

Cervix

Uterus (womb)

Vagina

FRONT VIEW

FEMALE SEXUAL SYSTEM

vagina and out of the body. This monthly event is called **menstruation** (this is what a woman means when she says she is "having her period") and lasts from three to six days. Although the fluid is red and contains blood (on the average about three tablespoonfuls), menstruation is not bleeding in the ordinary sense of the word. It is mainly the discarding of some blood and tissues that are now of no use. Menstruation signals the end of the current cycle.

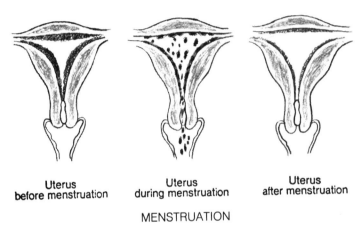

Uterus
before menstruation

Uterus
during menstruation

Uterus
after menstruation

MENSTRUATION

How can a girl know when she is about to have her first period? The "timetable" is different for each girl. In both boys and girls, generally somewhere between the ages of nine and eighteen, there occurs a period of rapid growth that we call a **growth spurt.*** It lasts about three years, and during the girl's time of greatest growth, her height increases from 2½ to 4½ inches in a single year. Girls generally begin their growth spurt about two years before boys. This means that from the ages of a little over eleven until about fourteen (but the ages may dif-

*A gland called the **pituitary gland,** located at the base of the brain, is the master gland or "time clock" that largely governs the bodily events of sexual and reproductive maturing in both girls and boys. The actions of the pituitary gland on the many other glands of the body are a complicated chemical process which it is not necessary to explain here. If you take a biology course, you'll learn more about it.

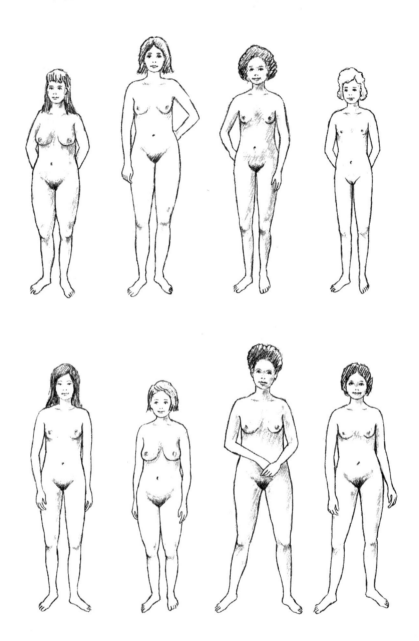

EIGHT NORMAL TEENAGE GIRLS OF THE SAME AGE

fer even more than this), girls go through a period when they are, on the average, a bit taller than boys of the same age. A girl's first menstruation may come at almost any time during her growth spurt, or sometimes even after it is over. Most often, however, it comes about three quarters of the way through the growth spurt.

On the average (but remember, most people aren't just at the average; there is great variation), about three to four years before a girl's first menstruation her breasts begin to swell. In most girls, the breasts become noticeable two or three years before menstruation. A year and a half to two and a half years before menstruation, **pubic hair** appears above her genitals, and about six months before, other hair appears under her arms. [The area of the genitals, including the lips (**labia**) enfolding the **clitoris,** is called the **vulva;** see the following drawing.]

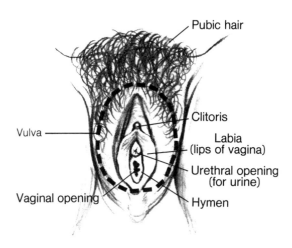

DETAILED VIEW OF FEMALE GENITAL AREA

A girl's first menstruation is the sign that she has reached puberty, that she is becoming capable of her part in producing a child—she can become **pregnant**. However, in many girls there is a gap of several months to a year or more between the first menstruation and the first ovulation. In other words, the first menstruation does not necessarily mean that a girl is immediately capable of having a baby. On the other hand, it is possible for a young girl to become pregnant even *before* her menstruation; that is, a few girls may ovulate for the first time before they ever menstruate.

Generally, the first menstruation occurs between the ages of eleven and fourteen. However, some girls menstruate as early as nine, and a few not until they are fifteen, sixteen, or seventeen. It is understandable that many girls worry about whether they are ahead of or behind their friends in physical development, but the worry is unnecessary. A girl is almost certain to be ahead of some and behind others. If she is worried, it is a simple matter for her to be examined by a **gynecologist**—a doctor who specializes in the health problems of women—for assurance that her development is normal, and for any needed treatment if it is not.

One way a girl can tell that she is going to have her period is to look for cervical **mucus** secretions at her vulva area, which occur several days before ovulation and then dry up. The secretions resemble raw egg white and make her vulva feel wet and slippery. A girl can expect to menstruate about two weeks after the mucus dries up.

When a girl begins to menstruate, it means that her body is now maturing, but not for several years will she be mature enough as a whole person, mind and body, to undertake the responsibilities of marriage and childbearing. Menstruation marks the beginning of **adolescence** for a girl. Adolescence is the period of perhaps eight years during which a girl is neither a child nor an adult, but a person on the way to becoming an adult.

Menstruation can be inconvenient, but it's a good healthy part of being a woman. When menstruation starts, many girls use a disposable pad or napkin to absorb the menstrual flow. It is made of cellulose or other absorbent material in a gauze covering and comes in two or three sizes. It can be held in place along the opening of the vagina by a sticky backing that clings to a girl's panty. Many girls use a different menstrual aid called a **tampon.** Tampons also come in different sizes. They are made of absorbent material shaped into a small roll for easy insertion into the vagina, where they absorb the flow. For health reasons, pads and tampons should be changed frequently, according to the instructions that come with them. If they are not changed regularly, at least every six hours, a rare disease called **toxic shock syndrome** may occur.

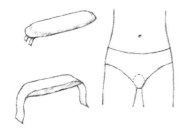

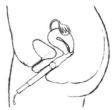

Tampon and device
for inserting
it into the vagina

MENSTRUAL PADS AND TAMPONS

Some girls may not be able to use a tampon at first because the entrance to the vagina is partly closed by a membrane called the **hymen.** (A membrane is a thin, sheetlike layer of living tissue.) However, if they start with a small-size

DIFFERENT TYPES OF HYMEN AT VAGINAL OPENING

tampon and slowly stretch the hymenal opening, most girls soon will be able to use this convenient menstrual aid.

Many people mistakenly believe that it is possible to tell whether or not a girl is a **virgin** (a female who has not had sexual intercourse) by whether her hymen is unbroken or broken. However, this is not a reliable sign, because in many girls an ample opening in the hymen develops quite naturally and without intercourse, or the hymen may even be almost entirely absent at birth.

When a girl is approaching her first **menstrual period,** it's a good time for her to talk with her mother or some other trusted person, in order to get good advice concerning the use of pads, napkins and tampons.

Occasionally, girls and women find the few days before and during menstruation difficult. Some may have pains in the abdomen or aches in the lower back as the muscles of the uterus contract to discard the unneeded lining. Some may also have headaches or feel depressed and edgy. Tears or temper may come rather easily. This is perfectly natural, and these feelings will generally go away in a day or two. Sometimes a girl needs the advice of a doctor to help her have a more comfortable menstrual period.

It may take more than a year for a girl's menstrual periods to become somewhat regular, but this should be no cause for worry. In many women the periods never become entirely regular, and for almost all women there are occasional times of irregularity.

A girl should lead her normal life during her period. She may participate in sports. If she swims, she should use a tampon. Cleanliness is important during menstruation, as at all other times. It is helpful if a girl bathes or showers every day and, as I have said, changes the pad or tampon at least every six hours, especially during the time when the flow is full.

Usually between ages forty-five and fifty-five a woman goes through a process called **menopause,** or change of life. At the end of this process, her ovaries discharge no more eggs and menstruation ceases. It does not mean the end of her sexual life—only that she can no longer bear a child. She can still enjoy sex; in fact, she may enjoy it even more now that there is no possibility of her becoming pregnant.

The man's sex organs and how they develop and work

Here now are the details about the sex organs of men. They consist of a complicated system of glands, tubes, and containers designed to manufacture the male reproductive cell, called the **sperm,** to store it, and to deliver it into the woman's body.

On the opposite page you see a drawing of a grown man. Next to it are two more-detailed drawings of his sexual parts, or **genitals.** You should refer to these diagrams as you read.

A man's most obvious sexual organ is his **penis,** which is usually about the length of a finger, although somewhat larger around. A small tube, the **urethra,** runs from the **bladder** down through the center of the penis. One purpose of this tube is to empty urine from the bladder. The other purpose is to provide a passageway for sperm, which I shall say more about later.

The end of a man's penis is covered by a sheath of skin called the **foreskin.** Some parents—especially Jews and Muslims, whose religions require it—have their infant sons **circumcised.** That is, the foreskin of the penis is removed by the doctor or specialist just after the baby's birth. This is a quick and simple surgical operation involving only the very tip of the penile skin. However, except when there are religious requirements, today most doctors think it is better to leave the penis uncircumcised, and the American Academy of Pediatricians agrees. Below are drawings of an uncircumcised penis and a

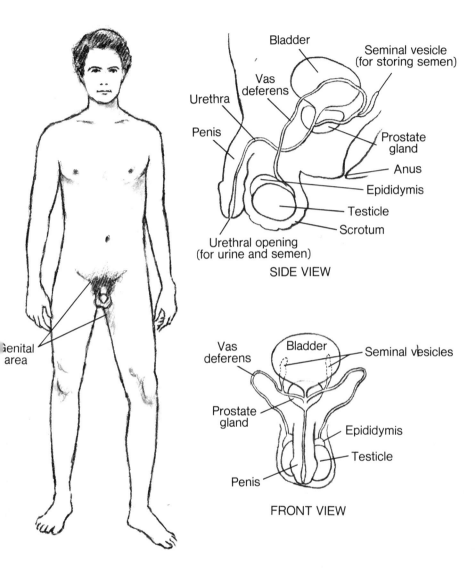

Bladder

Seminal vesicle
(for storing semen)

Vas
deferens

Urethra

Penis

Prostate
gland

Anus

Epididymis

Testicle

Scrotum

Urethral opening
(for urine and semen)

SIDE VIEW

Genital
area

Vas
deferens

Bladder

Seminal vesicles

Prostate
gland

Epididymis

Testicle

Penis

FRONT VIEW

MALE SEXUAL SYSTEM

circumcised one. As far as health and sexual life are concerned, it makes little or no difference whether a man's penis is circumcised or uncircumcised. It is important to push back the foreskin and wash the head of the penis regularly, however, if it has not been circumcised.

Under the man's penis hangs a sac of loose, (very soft and wrinkly) skin called the **scrotum,** which contains the two **testicles,** or **testes.** These oval-shaped glands, each about 1½ inches long in a grown man, are where sperm, the male reproductive cells, are made. Often one testis will hang lower than the other. Behind and against each testicle is a storage place, the **epididymis**—really a collection of about half a mile of tiny tubes—where the millions of sperm cells are matured as they pass through. Each sperm cell is shaped like a tadpole with a long, thin tail and is so small that five hundred of them placed end to end would take up only an inch. Sperm can be seen only through a microscope.

Uncircumcised   Circumcised

PENIS AND SCROTUM

From the epididymis the sperm cells travel through a long flexible tube, the **vas deferens** or spermatic duct, toward the **seminal vesicles,** which are two small storage pouches at the back of the **prostate gland.** The prostate secretes a thick, milky liquid that mixes with the sperm. This mixture is called **semen** and is stored in the seminal vesicles, the prostate, and the upper part of the vas deferens, ready to be discharged through the penis and to start the sperm on its way to the egg cell in the female.

When a man is sexually stimulated, and at some other times, a remarkable change occurs in his penis. This change is called an **erection;** it is caused by a quick flow of blood into the spongy tissues of the usually limp penis. The penis then grows firm and erect and increases in diameter and in length, becoming commonly from 5 to 8 inches long in a mature man. It stands out from the body at an angle and is then ready for sexual intercourse (see the next chapter), even though most erections in boys and men—and baby boys, too—subside without intercourse or any other sexual activity. The shape and angle of the erect penis differ from one man to another.

There is no relation between the size or length of a man's penis and his sexual power, and a penis that is small when limp increases much more during erection than does a penis that is large when limp. In addition, the size of the erect penis makes little difference in sexual pleasure, since a woman's vagina comfortably adjusts to accommodate any size penis, and the clitoris and most sensitive parts of the vagina are near the outside, where even the shortest erect penis can easily reach.

Most teenage boys and most men have frequent erections, both while awake and while asleep. These may be caused by reading or listening to music, by the nearness of a sexually attractive person, by thoughts or dreams about sex, or merely by the early morning need to urinate. As I have said, most erections end without any discharge of semen: The valves in certain veins open and allow the extra supply of blood to return to the main circulation system of the body. When a discharge of semen does occur, it is called an **ejaculation.** It comes as a series of quick, short spurts of the milky-white fluid. In most males, after the ejaculation, the penis rather quickly becomes limp again.

In a mature, healthy man each drop of semen contains tens of thousands of sperm cells, whose full name is **spermatozoa.** From 100 to 500 million spermatozoa are contained in the spoonful or so of semen discharged from the penis during an ejaculation. Yet small as it is, each single sperm cell may be capable of uniting with an egg cell inside the female and starting a new human life.

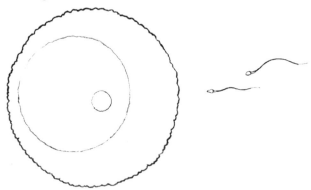

EGG AND SPERM CELLS SHOWING COMPARATIVE SIZES
(scale of both vastly enlarged)

Some people wonder if it is harmful for the semen to travel through the same passage in the penis as that used by the urine, and if semen and urine might get mixed together. This cannot happen. A small valve automatically shuts off the urine while ejaculation is taking place, and the sex glands secrete a special fluid to neutralize any remains of urine before the semen is ejaculated.

How can a boy know when he will begin to produce and ejaculate semen? This event occurs during a boy's adolescent growth spurt, just as the first menstruation comes during the growth spurt of a girl. (See the footnote on page 9 about the pituitary gland.) Different boys may begin and end their growth spurts at very different ages; in fact, some don't begin their spurt of growth until others have completed theirs. A boy's rapid increase in height may start anywhere between the ages of ten and sixteen and end between ages thirteen and eighteen. This does not mean that the boy has reached his full height at thirteen to eighteen, only that the period of extra-rapid increase ends somewhere during that period. In a boy's single year of peak growth, he may become 2½ to 5 inches taller.

There is great variation from boy to boy, but the first ejaculation of semen comes, on the average, about a year after his penis and testicles have started to grow noticeably, and at about the same time as his year of peak growth. One of the most reliable signs of approaching ejaculation is the appearance, just above the penis, of **pubic hair,** which at first is downy but gradually becomes darker, coarser, and curly. Usually somewhat later, hair also begins to grow in the armpits. About three to four months after the first curly pubic hair appears, the first ejaculation with semen comes, although, let me emphasize again, the length of time varies greatly from boy to boy. When a boy first ejaculates semen, we say that he has reached puberty and is entering adolescence.

In Chapter 3, I said that the average girl's growth spurt begins about two years earlier than the average boy's. However, there is a much smaller difference in time between the average girl's first menstruation and the average boy's first ejaculation. The difference is about six months. Thus, girls who may look quite grown up are often not so far ahead of boys who don't look very grown up, as far as the development of their sex organs goes.

Sometimes a boy's first ejaculation with semen will occur at night while he is asleep. He may be having a dream and will awaken to find that semen has been discharged onto his pajamas or the sheet. This is called a **nocturnal emission** (it means a nighttime sending out of semen) or "wet dream," and it is the body's way of getting rid of excess semen. A boy need not feel embarrassed if his mother or father sees evidence of

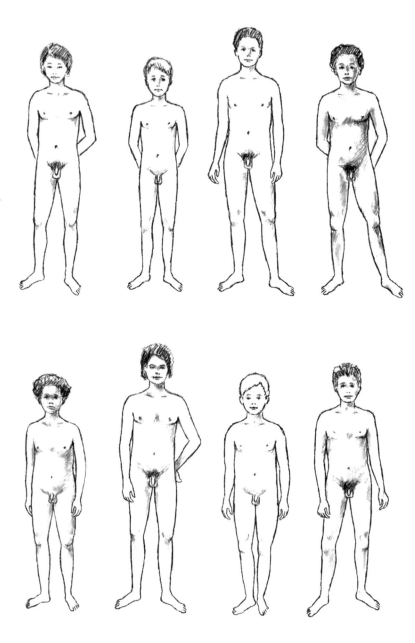

EIGHT NORMAL TEENAGE BOYS OF THE SAME AGE

his emission of semen. They will understand perfectly well what has happened and know that it is a sign that their son's body is now maturing.

More often, a boy's first ejaculation will come because he has been **masturbating**—rubbing his penis with his hand or against the sheets. Chapter 12 tells more about masturbation.

The change of voice that boys undergo in early adolescence usually begins a few months after the first ejaculation of semen, although there is great variation in the time. The change is caused by a rather sudden increase in the size of the voice box. This is a part of the young adolescent's spurt of growth.

It is perfectly normal for a boy to reach puberty as early as age ten or eleven, or perhaps not until he's fifteen or sixteen. As you can see from the drawings of eight teenage boys of the same age, there are great differences at this time of life. Many boys worry about whether they are ahead of or behind their friends, and this is understandable. However, the worrying is not necessary. They will almost certainly be ahead of some and behind others. By the time they are twenty or so, there will be very few important differences in physical sexual development among them.

The beginning of ejaculation at puberty does not mean that a boy has become a man. It does mean that he has become capable of making a female pregnant.

CHAPTER FIVE

Man and woman unite in sexual intercourse

In Chapter 3 you followed the path of the egg cell after it leaves the ovary. In Chapter 4 you read about how the sperm cells were made and discharged from the man's penis. Now it's time to explain how the sperm leaves the body of the man, enters the body of the woman, and, perhaps, meets the egg.

This process is called **sexual intercourse.** Another word for it is **coitus;** and when people speak or write about a man and a woman "going to bed together," "sleeping together," "having sex," "having relations," "making love," or, sometimes, "doing it," they are referring to sexual intercourse. There are two very common slang words for intercourse: *fuck* and *screw.* You should be very careful how you use these words, since many people are shocked or embarrassed by them (see pages 68–69). If you look up *intercourse* in a dictionary, you will find that its meaning includes the idea of exchange and communication. Thus sexual intercourse is a kind of communication, through sex, between two persons. When two people who are deeply in love have intercourse, they often exchange thoughts and feelings; they communicate their love for each other in an intimate and joyous way.

Some couples may have sexual intercourse several times a week, others perhaps only once or twice a month, whatever they choose for themselves. Intercourse and preparation for it may take anywhere from a few minutes to half an hour or more. Different couples have different styles. The couple might kiss, embrace, and caress many parts of each other's bodies. They might speak their love for each other. There are many other ways that they can enjoy this period of **foreplay**. After a time, their minds and bodies are ready for the act of coitus. The woman's vagina has become wet with a colorless fluid resulting from her sexual excitement. Meanwhile, and usually much more quickly, the man's penis has become erect so that, when the woman is ready, it enters her vagina easily. The man moves his penis in and out inside the vagina, and the woman may also move in various ways. The motions of intercourse cause friction against the concentration of nerve endings in the head of the penis and sometimes against similar nerve endings in the very sensitive clitoris (see the diagram on page 11). This stimulation of the penis, and of the clitoris and vagina, is the main physical cause of **orgasm** in men and women, and it gives both partners great pleasure.

After a time, then, each partner may reach orgasm, the climax of sexual pleasure, in a glorious spasm that is impossible to describe adequately in a few words. For the man, orgasm is the moment when the sperm is ejaculated in a series of quick spurts. During intercourse, the sperm is deposited inside the vagina close to the neck of the uterus (the **cervix**: see the diagram on page 8). For the woman, the orgasm involves a series of muscular contractions of the walls of the vagina. A man and woman seldom experience orgasm at the same moment. For each, the orgasm is accompanied by rapid, heavy breathing, sounds of delight, and other signs of an exciting climax.

Many women rarely or even never experience orgasm during intercourse, whereas men almost always do. Men do because the walls of the vagina automatically stimulate the head of the penis and this sets off the orgasm. But women are less likely to have an orgasm during intercourse because, no matter what position the partners use, the man's penis usually does not come in contact with the woman's clitoris, except as the movements of the penis may stimulate the clitoris indirectly during the motions of intercourse. Therefore, with many couples, so that the woman may enjoy orgasm, the man—or the woman herself—stimulates the clitoris before, during, or after intercourse.

As I have said, sexual intercourse is the way pregnancy begins. The man's orgasm and ejaculation of sperm are necessary to fertilize the egg (ovum). However, a woman generally ovulates about once a month whether or not she has an orgasm. There is no connection between female orgasm and ovulation. Some people have the idea that orgasm releases the ovum the way ejaculation releases the sperm, but this is wrong.

After the climaxes of intercourse, a couple who love and understand each other will often feel especially close and relaxed. They experience a sense of well-being and contentment together. In other words, although the physical pleasure of intercourse is intense, much more is involved than just bodily sensations. It involves a person's feelings, thoughts, and emotions. If intercourse is undertaken outside of a truly loving and caring relationship, then it can sometimes hurt one or both of the partners and their relationship. Within marriage, intercourse usually strengthens and intensifies the love that husband and wife feel for each other. (I discuss these important matters more fully in Chapter 13, "Some Ways That Sex Can Become a Problem," and Chapter 16, "Sex and Social Life.")

Often when a couple have intercourse for the first time, the experience is a disappointing one. It doesn't turn out to be the ecstasy that each was counting on. For the man, it may all be over too fast; for the woman, it may involve some discomfort, or she may not have experienced an orgasm. Sexual intercourse is something that loving couples learn how to enjoy more and more as they become more skilled and more aware of each other's feelings. If a man and woman learn how to tell each other, either by words or by signals that each learns to recognize, what feels good, what they like and do not like, then their pleasure in sex together increases. A man can learn to delay his orgasm until his partner becomes more ready for hers; a woman can learn to show her partner how to help her to have a climax, or she can learn to help herself, by stimulation of the clitoris and the area around it.

It is important, also, for the couple to feel relaxed and comfortable and unhurried together. Many couples do not enjoy intercourse as much as they might because they see it as something that must be accomplished—an act, even a task, to be performed—rather than a pleasure to be enjoyed. Yet if a woman does not feel like having an orgasm because she is tired, or if a man finds he is unable, from time to time, to keep his penis erect and to ejaculate, it need be no great thing. A loving exchange of feelings is good even if only one, or neither, of the partners has an orgasm.

There are many positions in human intercourse. The most common one is for the partners to lie front to front, with the man above the woman. But couples can enjoy a variety of pleasures by trying out different positions and different means of enjoyment.

If a woman wants to avoid difficulty and discomfort the first time she has intercourse, she may use tampons beforehand to dilate (enlarge) the opening in her hymen, or she may enlarge it gradually over a period of time by using her fingers, being very sure they are clean. In a few women the hymen is so strong and the opening so small that a doctor will think it wise to enlarge the vaginal entrance before the woman has intercourse. This is a simple and almost painless procedure.

Often, but not always, the first time a woman has intercourse, the stretching of the hymen opening may cause discomfort and slight bleeding. This is physically harmless.

We will continue to talk about human sexuality in Chapter 9, but right now let's find out more about the sperm and the egg.

CHAPTER SIX

Heredity: what is passed on to us by the sperm and the egg

Remember that two hundred egg cells placed side by side would take up only an inch. Five hundred sperm cells lined up head to tail would measure the same length. Yet each of these microscopically small cells contains many little structures called **chromosomes.** These chromosomes transmit a complicated code of directions. The code determines the **heredity** of the child that will be born if a sperm and an egg unite: the color of the hair, skin, and eyes; the shape of the nose; potential intelligence; and the thousands of other things that make this human being physically different from all other human beings. You know that children often look like their parents. All the resemblance is carried by the chromosomes in a single sperm and a single egg.

For a moment, let's consider a few details about how this code of heredity is carried. In each sperm cell and egg cell, small as it is, there are molecules of a chemical called **DNA.** Each molecule looks somewhat like a twisted ladder, weighs about one-trillionth (1/10,000,000,000,000) of an ounce, and contains many **genes.** In each gene of the DNA molecule is stored a set of chemical directions so complicated that to write them down in English would require several hundred volumes the size of a dictionary. Every cell in your body contains these same molecules. They are so small that if all the DNA molecules in all of the cells in all of the 4½ billion people now on the earth were piled close together like logs of wood, the whole pile would fit into a cubical box with an edge three sixteenths

(³⁄₁₆) of an inch long, like this: In a sense, you might say that all the people in the world could fit into that little box.

The science of heredity is called **genetics** (from the word "gene"), and what you are now and will become is determined partly by your genes and partly by your surroundings, called **environment**. There is more about this in later chapters.

CHAPTER SEVEN

From fertilization to birth of the baby

At the man's climax in intercourse, millions of sperm cells (100 to 500 million!), swimming in semen, are ejaculated from his penis into the woman's vagina near the mouth of the cervix. At once these microscopic sperm, whose rapidly lashing tails project them forward, begin a journey that takes from one to several hours. In their warm, moist environment, the sperm normally stay alive and are capable of fertilizing the egg cell for about two to five days, although sperm may be actively moving as long as a week after they are ejaculated.

Sperm appear to have no sense of direction, and they cannot see. They move about rapidly in a fairly random motion, not on a direct route. Some make their way up through the cervix into the uterus. Some of these, helped by contractions of the muscles of the uterus, enter the two fallopian tubes. They proceed up the tubes, where they may meet a mature egg cell traveling slowly in the opposite direction. If they do, they crowd around the ovum and hit against its wall until it weakens at one spot just enough to permit a single sperm cell to enter. At once the cell wall hardens and the other sperm are shut out. The successful one loses its tail; its head joins the nucleus of the egg. The rest of the sperm cells die very soon and are absorbed harmlessly into the woman's body. The moment of joining of sperm and egg is called **fertilization** or **conception**. The woman has conceived; she is pregnant.

It is important to understand that fertilization will not

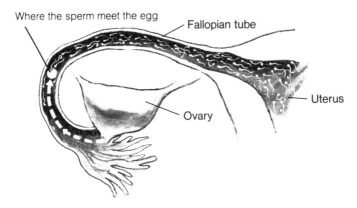

Where the sperm meet the egg

Fallopian tube

Uterus

Ovary

MOMENT OF FERTILIZATION
(scale of egg and sperm vastly enlarged)

occur every time a man and woman have intercourse—far from it. The sperm must arrive in the fallopian tube just when an egg is traveling through it. The sperm must be vigorous and the egg not too old—that is, not more than twelve to twenty-four hours out of the ovary.

It is the sperm cell that determines whether the child is to be a boy or a girl. The sex or **gender** depends on which of two types of sperm cell enters the ovum. If it is a sperm carrying a "Y" chromosome, the baby will be a boy; if it is an "X" chromosome, it will be a girl. Nothing that happens to the mother after fertilization can change the sex of the baby.

Since the thick lining of the uterus, the endometrium, now is needed for the fertilized egg to implant itself and grow in, it is not discarded, and the woman will not have any more menstrual periods until after the baby is born. Missing her period is usually the first sign to a woman that she may be going to have a baby. However, there are other reasons for delayed or missed periods, such as fatigue, excitement, nervousness, or change of diet or climate. Therefore, a woman usually should wait for a week or two beyond her normal time of menstruation before she decides that she is probably pregnant. Then if her period does not come, she will want to know for sure. Beginning about ten days after her missed period, a doctor or other specialist can tell with reasonable certainty by testing a sample of her urine. Also, there are now testing kits available without prescription that can be used at home, although they are not entirely reliable and can be misread. A woman can be more certain if she goes to a doctor or clinic to determine whether or not she is pregnant. There, blood tests are done that can detect pregnancy as early as twelve days after fertilization.

Other signs of pregnancy that some women may experience a bit later are enlargement and tingling of the breasts and "morning sickness," when they feel sick at the stomach, most often in the morning.

Once a woman is pregnant, her ovaries produce no more mature eggs until after the baby is born. Thus, when a woman has intercourse during pregnancy, no egg is there ready to be fertilized by a sperm, and there is no possibility of getting pregnant a second time.

Let's go back for a moment to the instant of fertilization. As soon as the egg is fertilized, it begins to divide and grow as it is moved on down the fallopian tube. As you know, it enters the uterus, and after a while implants itself in the uterine wall. This whole process takes several days (see diagram, page 33).

As you have read in Chapter 3, the uterus is ready to nourish the egg as it grows. Later, as it increases in size, the growing baby becomes surrounded by two strong coverings and is cushioned in fluid, which protects it from jolts and shocks.

The time between conception and the birth of the baby, when it is growing inside the womb of its mother, is called the period of **gestation**. This is the period during which the mother is said to be pregnant. In human beings pregnancy, or gestation, averages 266 days, or about eight and a half months, from the moment of fertilization. This is 280 days, or about

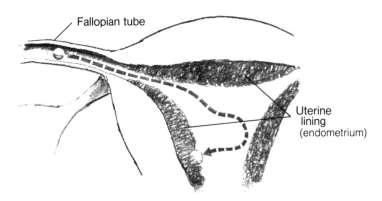

IMPLANTATION OF FERTILIZED EGG IN LINING OF UTERUS
(scale of egg vastly enlarged)

nine months, from the beginning of the last menstrual period. The gestation period often is spoken of as being divided into three **trimesters** of three months each—the first, second, and third trimesters. The baby, first called an **embryo** and later a **fetus,** grows by **cell division,** from one cell at conception to over 200 billion cells at the time of birth. As they multiply, these cells organize themselves in complex ways. They **differentiate** themselves into just what is needed to make the thousands of parts of the human body, from heart and brain to toenail and eyelash.

During this process, how does the baby receive nourishment from the mother? Early in pregnancy, a structure forms in the uterus that enables the embryo to receive the food, water, and oxygen it needs. This structure is called the **placenta.** It is a thick disk-shaped collection of blood vessels. The nourishment passes from the mother's bloodstream to the growing baby through the placenta, which is connected to the baby by means of a long ropelike cord, the **umbilical cord** (see the drawing, page 39). The cord also contains many tiny blood vessels, which at one end intertwine with (but do not join) those of the placenta. Through the blood vessels in this cord the embryo receives its nourishment and disposes of its waste products such as carbon dioxide. But the mother's blood does not enter the embryo. The embryo manufactures its own blood.

The human embryo at first resembles embryos of other animals. For a short time it has the beginning of gills, as in fish embryos, although they are not really gills; later it appears to have a tail; still later its body is covered with fine, downy hair.

At four weeks the embryo is about ¼ inch long (as long as this: ___ but somewhat curled). It no longer has gill-like ridges, but it still has a tail; and it would be difficult to tell it apart from the embryo of a fish, turtle, chicken, or any other animal.

At eight weeks (two months), the embryo is about 1 inch long, and it would take about five hundred such embryos to weigh a pound. Even though it is this small, it already has a large-looking head with the beginnings of eyes, ears, a nose, and a mouth. Its heart is now pumping blood through its small body.

At twelve weeks (three months), the embryo has made a great spurt of growth and is now about 4 inches long, although it weighs only about ⅓ ounce. It would take only about fifty embryos to weigh a pound.

At sixteen to seventeen weeks (four months), it has grown to be 6 inches long and weighs ⅓ pound. Its bones have begun to develop, and its arms and legs can move. The mother may now be able to feel the first faint flutter of activity, called **quickening.** When she feels this she knows with a new certainty that a live being is inside her. By this time the being is called a fetus, no longer an embryo.

At twenty-one weeks (five months), the fetus would be about 10 inches long if its legs were stretched out straight, and it weighs about ¾ pound. Its body is now covered with downy hair.

At twenty-five weeks (six months), the fetus is about a

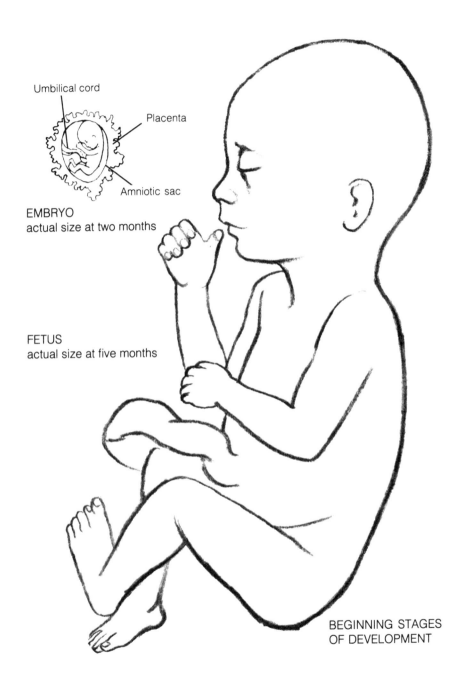

Umbilical cord

Placenta

Amniotic sac

EMBRYO
actual size at two months

FETUS
actual size at five months

BEGINNING STAGES
OF DEVELOPMENT

foot long and weighs perhaps 1¼ pounds. It is beginning to lose the hair that covered its body and looks quite a lot like a human baby now, except that it is thin and has not yet begun to store up fat.

At about twenty-nine weeks (seven months), it is 14 inches long and probably weighs over 2 pounds. The body hair has all gone.

By twenty-five to twenty-six weeks, the baby has matured enough so that if it is born ahead of time it has a 10 percent chance to live, if well cared for in an intensive-care nursery. By twenty-seven to twenty-eight weeks, the chances are 50 percent. By twenty-nine to thirty weeks (about 7 months), its chances for survival rise to over 80 percent. Such a baby is called **premature,** since it is born before the full term of nine months.

During months eight and nine the fetus grows to an average weight of 7 or 8 pounds. At the end of the 266-day gestation period, it is ready to be born, all 200 billion cells of it.

In the last three or four months of pregnancy, as the fetus increases in size, things get a bit crowded inside the abdomen of the mother. Of course, the uterus is entirely separate from the stomach (in spite of what some children are erroneously told about the baby growing "in its mother's tummy"), but as the uterus expands, the bladder and stomach and all the other organs are pressed upon. That explains why an expectant mother needs to urinate more often than usual and eats smaller, more frequent meals. (See the drawings on pages 39 and 41.)

It seems a miracle that the remarkable plan of growth for the body was already contained in the DNA of the original fertilized cell. There was a set pattern that could not be changed. Not only was it determined in advance that what would be born was a human being, and not a mouse or cow or elephant, but also determined were all of the thousands of inherited traits that make a person truly the product of his or her parents and ancestors.

You may wonder what the effect on the fetus is if the pregnant woman smokes, drinks alcohol, or takes drugs. Studies of these effects continue to be made, but we do know that

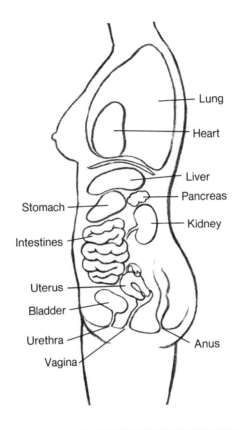

NORMAL POSITION OF WOMAN'S BODY ORGANS

mothers who smoke tend to have smaller babies and more complications than those who do not. Also, when the mother smokes, the heartbeat of the fetus speeds up somewhat. When the mother drinks alcohol, the baby's movements inside the uterus are slowed down while the alcohol is in the mother's bloodstream, and it is well established that heavy drinking by a woman during pregnancy is, in many cases, very harmful to her baby, both at birth and quite likely through its life. Indeed, some babies of alcoholic mothers are born with a disorder called **fetal alcohol syndrome,** which causes physical

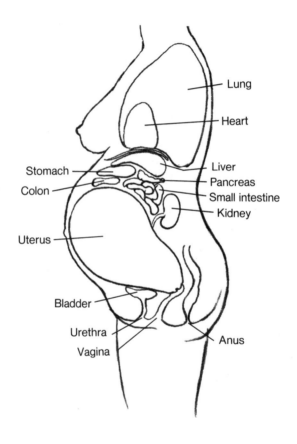

DISPLACEMENT AND COMPRESSION
OF BODY ORGANS DURING PREGNANCY

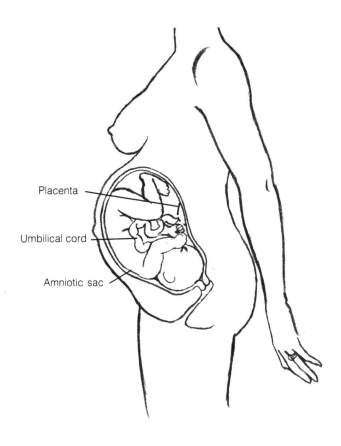

Placenta

Umbilical cord

Amniotic sac

WOMAN IN HER NINTH MONTH OF PREGNANCY

deformities and mental retardation. It is the third leading cause of birth defects in the U.S.

Marijuana also has a temporary effect on the baby though it is not known whether it is harmful. However, "hard" drugs are very injurious to the baby, especially heroin. As the mother becomes addicted to heroin, the baby also becomes addicted, and after it is born it goes through painful and serious withdrawal symptoms, just as an adult does when taken off the drug.

One birth in every ninety or so produces twins. (One in about every eight thousand produces triplets.) Twins are formed in two ways. One way is when each of the mother's two ovaries releases an egg at about the same time, or one ovary releases two eggs. Thus, each fallopian tube contains an egg, or one tube contains two eggs, and when the sperm cells enter the tubes, both eggs are fertilized. Each egg becomes separately implanted in the uterus, and each embryo has its own placenta. Twins who start this way are really ordinary brothers or sisters whose original egg cells just happened to be fertilized at the same time and who were therefore born at the same time. They may be of the same or opposite sex, and they do not look any more alike than brothers and sisters born at different times. They are called **fraternal twins.**

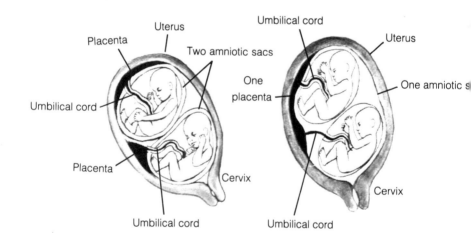

Left FRATERNAL TWINS (from two eggs; two placentas; sexes may differ)   *Right* IDENTICAL TWINS (from one egg, divided; single placenta; same sex)

The other way twins can occur is for the original fertilized cell, after implanting itself, to divide once into two separate parts and for each embryo then to develop independently. These single-egg twins are always of the same sex since they were started by the same sperm cell, and usually they look so much alike that they are hard to tell apart. They are called **identical twins.**

Much rarer are triplets, quadruplets, and quintuplets, who are usually the products of two or more eggs. Triplets most commonly result from two eggs, one of which divides to produce a pair of identical twins while the other egg produces a single infant.

CHAPTER EIGHT

How a baby is born and what a newborn is like

In just a little less than nine months after the baby is **conceived** (the egg fertilized), it is ready to be born. The mother's first signal that the time for birth has come is usually the start of **contractions** of the strong muscles of the uterus, accompanied by a dull ache or sensation of tightening as the contractions increase in power. (All muscles do their work by contracting.) At first these contractions are spaced perhaps fifteen minutes to half an hour apart, but when they begin to come every five to ten minutes, the mother should be taken to the hospital, or the doctor or **midwife** who will help her with the birth, perhaps at home, should be called in. (A doctor who specializes in the care of pregnant women is called an **obstetrician;** the midwife is a person, usually a nurse, especially trained to help in childbirth.)

The muscular contractions are called **labor,** and a woman who is about to bear a child is said to be in labor. Giving birth to a child is very hard work. It can also be painful, but often much of the discomfort can be avoided by the expectant mother who has conditioned her body for childbirth and who understands what is happening during birth well enough so that she can help guide the process, knowing when and how to push and when and how to relax, as well as how to communicate her needs and feelings to the doctor or midwife so that they can help her. Training courses are available to help women have a good experience of childbirth. Often their husbands share in the training so that they can be a source of support, help, and encouragement.

The discomfort of a woman in childbirth is perfectly natural, being caused by the powerful muscles that push out the baby. Many women prefer to have an anesthetic, which relieves the discomfort. Other women would rather be fully conscious while bearing a child, with only a mild anesthetic or none at all. Understanding what the experience of childbirth involves can relieve fear and anxiety, and this relief helps relax the muscles around the vagina, and particularly around the cervix, which must dilate, or stretch, to permit passage of the baby. Understanding makes the mother more relaxed, which increases the ease of the birth and helps speed the arrival of the baby.

The average length of labor for a mother producing her first child is between nine and eleven hours from the time the first regular contractions are felt. Some babies come much more quickly, others more slowly. The time for mothers who have given birth before is usually shorter, averaging around six hours.

During labor, the covering membranes that enclosed the baby usually break by themselves. Then the **amniotic fluid** they contained, which had acted as a cushion for the baby, flows out through the vagina. Sometimes labor is progressing well but the membranes haven't broken. In such cases the doctor uses a little hook to painlessly pinch an opening so that the fluid will come out and the period of labor be shortened. After this "rush of waters," as it is called, and toward the end of labor, the baby is transported through the vagina and out into the world by a series of pushes by the uterus. The head usually comes first, and it is usually a tight fit. But at the time of birth the baby's head is still somewhat soft and compressible enough not to be damaged, and it serves well to open the way for the rest of the body. The doctor or midwife is waiting to guide the head gently as it emerges and to guide the baby out easily as the birth is completed. After a minute or so, the doctor clamps and cuts the umbilical cord. This process is painless, since the cord contains no nerves. Your **navel,** or belly button, is the small scar and indentation that shows where the umbilical cord was attached, linking you to the placenta inside your mother.

After the baby is born, the uterus goes on contracting, but less vigorously, and in a few minutes the placenta and the two coverings that were protecting the baby emerge. These are called the **afterbirth** and are disposed of.

At birth the baby is on its own for the first time, and its first job is to start breathing in air—something it did not need to do (and could not do, floating in fluid) inside the uterus. It is helpful for the doctor or midwife to suction out the baby's nose and throat with a rubber bulb syringe or a suction machine to make it easier for the baby to start breathing. After its first breaths, the baby is likely to utter a small, high cry, which is a clear signal to the mother that she has delivered a child. A new person is out in the world.

Many boys and girls, having seen babies a few weeks or months old and knowing how cute and pretty they look, are a bit disappointed and even shocked when they see a newborn baby. (So are some mothers and fathers.) Usually a newborn is not at all beautiful, or even cute. It is wrinkly, splotchy, and often quite red. The baby's face may be swollen and look troubled, stupid, or even worn out, and in general it doesn't seem to be much of an addition to the family. But we have to remember that the process of getting itself born may have been fairly difficult for the baby. However, its color soon becomes normal, and its skin gets to look more skinlike. In less than a month, the baby will be cute and desirable-looking, and even a day or two after birth can work wonders.

Newborns can see enough to tell light from dark, but things are blurry to them at first until their eyes get used to focusing. They can taste, and they can feel pain and pressure. They do not like loud noises or the sensation of falling. Babies

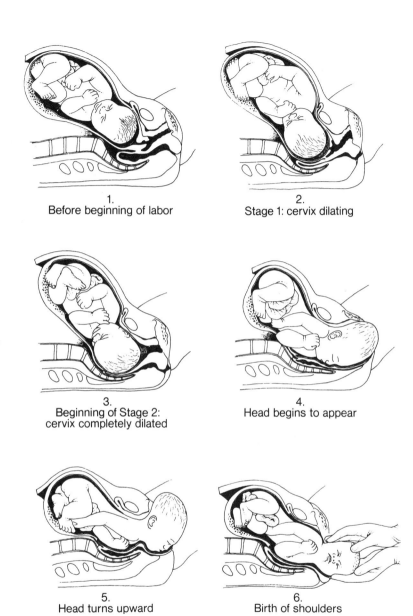

1.
Before beginning of labor

2.
Stage 1: cervix dilating

3.
Beginning of Stage 2:
cervix completely dilated

4.
Head begins to appear

5.
Head turns upward

6.
Birth of shoulders

BIRTH OF BABY

quickly learn that the way to get what they need is to cry. Many babies do a lot of crying during the first month, whether they need something or not, especially if their parents don't hold and cuddle them very much. Holding and cuddling is very important for babies.

An activity the newborn does very well is sucking. It has very strong sucking muscles and a little pad of fat in each cheek to help it. The baby will suck on anything that is put near its mouth. Its mother has just the right equipment for it to suck on. At the tip of each of her breasts is a **nipple,** and inside the breasts are glands that manufacture milk and a network of small tubes that bring the milk to the nipple when the baby sucks.

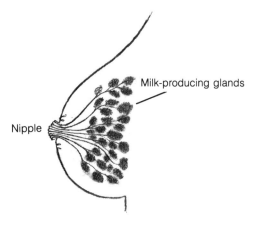

Milk-producing glands

Nipple

FEMALE BREAST

For the first day or two after the birth, the fluid from the mother's breasts, called **colostrum,** is slight in amount, yellowish, and watery. This is just what the baby needs. Colostrum contains some food and also special substances that help protect the baby from possible infections to which it is exposed now that it is in the world. The baby sucks actively even though it doesn't get much, but such suckling stimulates the breast glands to make milk that is more nutritious.

Mother's milk is an ideal baby food: It is clean, safe, and digestible, with just the right proportions of protein, fats, carbohydrates, minerals, and vitamins. For a baby, being held close and nursing at its mother's breast provides the feeling of warmth and closeness that it needs, and it is also pleasant and healthy for the mother, too.

There are a good many mothers who do not wish, or do not feel able, to nurse their babies. These babies are fed from a bottle that has a rubber nipple and contains a special formula similar to breast milk, and they can grow to be as sturdy and healthy as a breast-fed baby, especially if the father or mother holds the baby in his or her arms lovingly while the child sucks from the bottle.

CHAPTER NINE

Human sex and animal sex: some major differences

The main function of sex in nature is **reproduction,** that is, producing babies and carrying on the species, whether the species be birds, bees, rabbits, hamsters, hippopotamuses, gorillas, or human beings. Nothing in nature could be more important, and that is why sex is so attractive and the drive for it so urgent.

However, there are important differences between sex in most animals and sex in human beings. One difference is this: In most animals, except for some of the higher apes, **copulation,** or mating, usually takes place only when the female is in **heat**—that is, when she is ovulating and when copulation is likely to cause pregnancy. When she is in heat, she gives forth certain scents or other signs that tell the male she is ready to copulate. The male then becomes sexually aroused (he "ruts" or becomes "**rutty**"), and the mating takes place. At no other time is the female willing to copulate, and at that time the male is very responsive. Thus the main result of copulation in animals is reproduction. Of course, animals do not "know" this. They copulate because they feel an urge to do so.

In human females, on the other hand, there is no such thing as heat. Most women usually do not even know when they have ovulated and have an egg that is ready to be fertilized. (They can be taught to be aware, however. See "Natural Family Planning," pages 78–80.) Women do feel a greater desire for intercourse at some times than at others, but not necessarily at the time when they are most likely to conceive. Women do not give forth any special strong scent; their bodies do not advertise their readiness, as do the bodies of other animals. Further, for the human male there is no definite season when he is "rutty," although at some times he may feel more sexual desire than at others.

Thus, human sexual desire has relatively little relationship to whether or not a baby is likely to be produced at a given time. Most sexual intercourse between human beings takes place because of the desire, pleasure, joy, and love that are a part of it, rather than because of the need to produce children.

Sexual intercourse between a man and a woman, as I have said, can be and usually is a beautiful, loving, joyous thing. If the couple love and care for each other, their physical pleasure and sense of deep relationship can give them real ecstasy. On the other hand, it is not always so, and much depends on how the couple are feeling toward each other at the time and how they feel about their own lives. Their feelings also depend quite a lot on their surroundings.

The basic difference between human and animal sex arises out of the facts that I have described. Human beings are able to decide when they are going to engage in sexual activity; most animals have the decision made for them by **instinct,** by what is born into them, not by what they learn or think about. *Human beings are responsible for their sex life; animals are not.* There is a great variation in human sex life—variation from country to country, from culture to culture, from group to group, from person to person. There is no such variation within a species of animals. Dogs mate in the same way whether they are in India, France, Brazil, or the United States. Animal sex is only a matter of body. Human sex may seem to be simple, but in reality it is very complex. This is because our personalities, our emotions, our minds, and our upbringings are always involved. (I know a sex education teacher who says that our main sex organ is between our ears—that is, our brain!)

And there is yet another major difference. When animals in nature become sexually mature, they begin at once to copulate and reproduce their kind. And when young are produced by animals, the period during which the parents must provide care for them is generally quite short, usually less than a year. For example, with dogs and cats it is only several weeks. Human beings, on the other hand, are responsible for the care of their young from fifteen to twenty years, or more—longer than any animal (including chimpanzees, among which the child travels with its mother for seven to twelve years). Even after human beings reach puberty, it may still be another eight to ten years, or even longer in our culture, before they are ready to earn a living, establish a home, and take care of children of their own—in other words, to be responsible for the possible consequences of intercourse. As the well-known minister and social leader Jesse Jackson says, "You're not a man because you can make a baby. It takes a man to raise one. Girls can have a baby, but it takes a woman to raise one." This is something that all of us, boys and girls, parents and teachers, need to think about. (See Chapter 14, "Contraception," and Chapter 16, "Sex and Social Life.")

Let me repeat: The typical lower animal has little sexual freedom; it is limited by its seasons and driven by its instincts to copulate almost automatically. For it, the patterns are all set up in advance; there is little learning or choice. The animal's sex life is directly linked to reproduction. But men and women have much freedom of choice; they must decide what to do and what not to do. They depend greatly on what they are taught and how they learn it. They are *responsible* for their choices and decisions: they must take the consequences, good or bad. Therefore it is extremely important that they have enough knowledge, sense, and consideration to foresee those consequences and to act accordingly.

Thus human love and sex can result in pleasure and joyous satisfaction. Or the result can be a great sorrow and unhappiness if men and women are not considerate of each other in their sex lives and do not take responsibility for the result. To *become* a father or a mother is not very difficult, once you have reached puberty. To be a *good* father or mother, however, is not so simple. Being a good parent requires maturity, judgment, and lasting love. And it requires the commitment of both the father and the mother to the child and to each other. Then the child can grow up in a warm, supporting family.

CHAPTER TEN

Sex differences between women and men—and some similarities

We are now ready to go more deeply into the subject of sex differences between men and women—into human **sexuality.** "Sexuality" means more than "sex." It means all that goes with being a man or being a woman, a boy or a girl. It means the sexual part of one's personality. Authorities who have studied sex differences do not agree on the extent to which these differences are inborn or are created by the environment, that is, by the society we live in.

Before we think about differences between men and women, we should remember that there are at least two great similarities: First, as human beings, we are much more like one another than we are like any other animal or either sex. We speak and write language, we think complicated thoughts, we can remember the past and project ourselves into the future. We have imagination; we enjoy planning, and loving, and seeing ourselves as parts of the universe. Both male and female human beings are *conscious of themselves* and *conscious of others* in ways that, as far as we know, no other animals are. The second great similarity is physical: As human beings, both men and women can enjoy varieties of sexual activity and the ultimate sexual pleasure of orgasm with a degree of conscious awareness that animals, as far as we know, do not have, except possibly for some of the higher apes.

As for the differences, when we compare the sexuality of men and women, it is important to remember that a woman is more than just a non-man and a man is more than just a non-woman, and that every woman is different from every other woman and every man different from every other man.

Sexuality in Men

As a boy matures sexually, the sexual thoughts in his mind and feelings in his body are often quite definite and strong. They may be aroused rather quickly, and the arousal may be quite involuntary. The physical feelings are strongest in his penis, which becomes erect, and they sometimes make him desire an ejaculation.

However, most erections end without ejaculation. As boys grow up and become more mature emotionally as well as physically, they are able to understand that a sexual experience like intercourse is not something to be sought lightly or selfishly. When it is part of an expression of tenderness, caring, and commitment, it can be a deeply moving experience. Boys and men can combine their intelligence, their emotions, and their sexuality to help create relationships based on love, understanding, and caring. Girls can, too.

Sexuality in Women

A woman's sexuality tends to be somewhat different from a man's. Generally her sexual feelings are stirred more slowly, less often, and somewhat less sharply than those of men. However, once aroused, women's feelings are just as powerful and pleasurable. For many complicated reasons, women want intercourse less at some times than at others, and it is especially important to most women that giving and receiving love and affection be a part of lovemaking. (It's important for men, too.)

The sexual nature of women helps to make them understanding, considerate, and affectionate, and it is a great force in creating deep and satisfying human relationships. The sexual nature of men can well do the same.

Too often a man thinks that a woman reacts—or should react—just as he does, and a woman often does not understand the suddenness of a man's reaction. Understanding their sexual differences and lovingly considering them will help a man and a woman to be happy together. In the nineteenth and early twentieth centuries, especially in England and the United States, it was widely thought that men were supposed to enjoy sex and women were supposed to just endure it. There are still some people who believe a woman is not quite "nice" if she really enjoys sex. However, over most of the history of humankind, both men and women have known that the sexual experience can give intense pleasure, and that sex is not something that a man does *to* a woman or that a woman does *for* a man, but that each does for and with the other. A woman's orgasm is as strong and definite and exciting as a man's, and may be even stronger. Also, her orgasm may last longer than a man's, and she may have several orgasms in rather quick succession, which most men cannot have. Sexual activity at its best is a mutual exchange of pleasure, which includes caring about the pleasure of the other person.

Sexuality Is More Than Bodies

People express their sexuality in many different ways. Sexual intercourse and the steps leading up to it are only some of them. Sexuality is also expressed through clothing, conversation, manners, interests, education, cooking, recreation, daily work—in fact, most aspects of daily life. A person does what he or she does mainly as a person, it is true, but also as a boy or a girl, or as a man or a woman.

If you think back to your early childhood, you will probably remember that your parents treated you as a boy or as a girl, not only as a person. The words they spoke to you, the toys they gave you, the games they played with you, the clothes they dressed you in, the things they punished and rewarded you for—all of these things and many more—helped to develop the ways you express your sexuality, helped to establish your **gender identity** (whether you consider yourself to be male or female), helped to make you a boy or a girl with what is generally accepted as the personality of a boy or a girl.

Men and women tend to differ, therefore, in their feelings, desires, and personalities largely because they have been *taught* these differences. The differences may not be as immediately obvious as the differences in their bodies, but they are deep-seated and important. In general, until fairly recently anyway, most people have thought of a typical boy as being vigorous and aggressive, of a typical girl as being sweeter and gentler than a boy and having a greater desire to please others. A father has been expected to earn a living for his family and to provide manly companionship for his wife and children. A mother, even when she helps earn a living for the family as so many women now do, usually is expected to provide loving care for her children, to manage the household, and to be a source of tenderness and womanly love. Men and women can function well together in this way. And when they do, the result is a delight.

In recent years, however, there has been a strong desire on the part of many people not to be so molded by these expected **sex roles**—our society's ideas of how male and female ought to behave. Increasingly, we have come to accept and encourage husbands and wives sharing more equally the tasks of making a living and making a home. We recognize that some girls are aggressive and ambitious and some boys are gentle and accepting, and that this is all right. People have come more and more to want to be free, *free to be themselves*, whichever sex they may belong to. They are less willing to play unthinkingly the role of man or woman that our society tends to encourage. We are learning that in each of us, in differing degrees, there is some of what we think of as the masculine and some of what we think of as the feminine. This is fortunate because it makes it easier for men and women to understand each other. Remember, most of us have more similarities as human beings than we have differences as men and women. Some will find satisfaction and pleasure in living the sexual roles that society has traditionally expected of them. Others will find new relationships that are more satisfying to them.

Obviously, however, body differences do make substantial differences in the lives of men and women, especially those who marry and have families. The woman is the one who goes through the period of pregnancy and who gives birth to the baby; the man can't. The woman is the only one who can nurse the baby, if the baby is to be breast-fed. Also, men generally (not always) are larger and stronger than women, so any work requiring heavy physical effort can usually be more easily done by men.

For thousands of years, these body differences between men and women have made for differences in their lives. The pattern originated in primitive societies. Women became pregnant frequently; they were tied more closely to their homes than were men. Women had no choice but to carry, bear, and be the main care providers for the children. Men, on the other hand, because they were not carrying suckling infants, were the ones who had the time and energy to go off on longer cooperative hunting expeditions and bring home the meat the family and tribe needed. Meat was most often the high-prestige food. However, it was the women, along with their children, who foraged for edible plants and fruits. And anthropologists now estimate that, despite the importance given to hunters, it was the women who provided about 80 percent of the needed food. At any rate, over thousands of years the pattern of man, the hunter, and woman, the homebody, developed. Despite modern changes in attitude, this pattern remains the most common one the world over.

There is another way that body differences cause men and women to differ. This is in the chemicals, called **hormones,** that the glands in men's and women's bodies secrete into their bloodstreams. This subject is very complicated and not yet fully understood, but to take just one example, it is known that men's testicles secrete a hormone called **testosterone,** and that this hormone is a cause not only of the so-called **secondary sex characteristics** like the beard and larger, stronger body of a man, but also helps to cause vigorous behavior. Women's bodies also manufacture testosterone (the adrenal glands, which both men and women have, are the manufacturers), but normally much less of it than does the body of the typical male.

Two hormones produced *only* by women (by their ovaries) are **estrogen** and **progesterone.** Estrogen helps produce female sex characteristics and affects the way a woman's menstrual cycle works. Progesterone is the female "pregnancy hormone." It governs the preparation of the uterus to receive the fertilized egg and helps maintain the pregnancy. It also helps prepare a woman's breasts to produce milk.

So the long history of the human race, the different proportions and kinds of hormones in men's and women's bodies, and the facts of pregnancy and childbirth have resulted in certain deeply established differences in men and women. But these differences, which used to rule our lives, are not nearly as powerful as they were. Modern civilization has made it possible for both men and women to be more free to become the sort of people they want to be, with much less forced dependence on sexual and physical differences.

With this greater freedom comes greater responsibility and complexity. It is often difficult for us to know how to deal with our sexual feelings, whether toward people of the opposite sex or toward those of our own sex. It may also be difficult to deal with questions we may have about our gender identity and how to express it. None of us, and especially no young person, should hesitate to discuss our sexual feelings with a knowledgeable person if we would like to understand them better or are bothered by them and want to try to change them or adjust better to them. We should never have to feel "stuck" with our problems or with emotions that cause us discomfort.

CHAPTER ELEVEN

Homosexuality—being "gay"

Some people prefer sexual partners of their own sex and are not especially sexually attracted to people of the other sex—although, like anyone, they may be attracted to people of either sex in many ways other than sexually. Such people are called **homosexual.** They often refer to themselves, and are referred to by others as being "gay." Gay people look just the same as heterosexuals unless they choose, as they do at times, to look, dress, and act differently.

The word "homosexual" means "having to do with the same sex." (The first part of the word comes from the Greek *homos*, meaning "same," not from the Latin *homo*, meaning "man.") The opposite of homosexual is **heterosexual,** "having to do with the other sex" (from the Greek *heteros*, "other"). Heterosexuals are often called "straight," as distinguished from "gay." Female homosexuals are usually called **lesbians.** The name comes from the Greek island of Lesbos, where in ancient times many of the inhabitants were women who enjoyed a homosexual way of life together.

There are many people who are not completely homosexual or completely heterosexual but are **bisexual** (*bi-* comes from Latin and means "having to do with two"). They are people who are attracted either way, heterosexually or homosexually.

People often ask: What causes some individuals to prefer homosexual love and others to prefer heterosexual? Because of the incomplete state of our knowledge, there is as yet no single theory on which all scientists and doctors agree. Certainly it is not a simple matter. There is fairly general agreement, however, that a homosexual or heterosexual orientation is a way of being that is established very early in life, possibly before we are born.

Quite a few boys and girls when they enter puberty, or even earlier, feel strongly attracted to members of their own sex. For a while, most boys usually much prefer to associate with other boys, and girls with other girls. With some, these friendships are close and intense. They occasionally involve sexual experiences such as kissing or caressing, or masturbating together. But such experiences do not necessarily mean that those who participate in them are homosexuals, for most adolescents who engage in them go on to form heterosexual relationships.

Sometimes, also, a younger boy develops a special, intense fondness for a man, perhaps a teacher, a coach, or an older boy, and girls can experience the same sort of feeling toward a woman or older girl whom they admire. It is usually a one-way feeling; the older person probably does not feel the same way and may even be unaware of the special emotion of the younger person. Ordinarily, the boy or girl develops other interests after a time, and the intense feeling passes. This warm admiration for a more mature person of the same sex can have a beneficial effect on the development of the character and personality of a young teenager, if it leads him or her to strive for the admired qualities.

It is impossible to say how many people would openly express themselves through a mainly homosexual style of life if they felt perfectly free to do so. Surveys suggest that perhaps as many as 10 percent would, and probably more men than women. Many heterosexuals think that homosexuals have chosen to be homosexual, but most gay people know that it is not a matter of choice. It is what they are. Therefore the question of whether homosexuality is bad or good is a pointless one. Homosexuality exists just as heterosexuality does.

In society today many homosexuals choose to hide, or feel forced to hide, their homosexuality from the rest of the world. The reason for this is that life for homosexuals quite often is made difficult because so many people condemn them as strange and bad. This makes it hard for many homosexuals to have positive feelings about themselves. Also, it is sometimes more difficult for homosexuals than for others to get or keep good jobs or to be accepted as friends by heterosexual people. Those who discriminate against homosexuals in this way are displaying what is sometimes called **homophobia**: a strong, unreasoning fear of homosexuality. It is not unlike racial or religious prejudice. Despite the effects of homophobia in our society, however, many homosexual and bisexual men and women are happy and satisfied and successful. They are found in all walks of life—the sciences, engineering, construction work, the arts, sports, business management, and labor, to mention only a few.

Homosexual leaders and many others use the slogan "Gay is good." They have organized into hundreds of groups around the country, some on school and college campuses. Together, these groups are known as the "gay liberation movement." This movement encourages homosexuals to "come out," freely to enjoy their style of life, and to fight discrimination against homosexuals.

Gay people feel that they should be able to express themselves just as heterosexuals do—by holding hands in public, dancing together at a party, or introducing their family to someone they love. But they find that it still takes great courage in our antihomosexual society for them to do these simple, human things. They say that it is not homosexuality that is the problem so much as the bigotry and discrimination that gay men and lesbians must face. They urge all people, straight and gay, to uphold the right of gay people, along with all people, to live in ways that are fulfilling for them and harmless to others.

CHAPTER TWELVE

Masturbation

Masturbation means rubbing or stroking the genitals in order to have an orgasm. A boy does it by rubbing his penis, especially the head of the penis, with his hand or perhaps with or against some other object; a girl does it by stroking her clitoris or the area around it, or by pressing her thighs together rhythmically. Masturbation begins when very young children learn that they get a pleasurable feeling by handling their genitals. However, it is not limited to the young. Many men and women go on masturbating from time to time throughout their lives. Both married and unmarried people masturbate, and people can masturbate alone or together, heterosexually or homosexually. Of course there is certainly nothing wrong with *not* masturbating. However, the person who has never masturbated is an exception.

People sometimes talk and write about masturbation as a problem of sex. It really isn't a problem except as thinking makes it so. Unfortunately, some people believe that masturbation is harmful and are worried about boys and girls who masturbate. This is especially true among people who belong to religious groups that consider it to be a sin or a moral disorder. If a young person who masturbates lives closely with others who believe it is evil, he or she will probably feel guilty and ashamed. And, of course, when babies or very little girls or boys are punished for playing with their genitals, they get the idea that it's a bad thing.

Then there are those who say that masturbation may not

be so bad if you don't do it "too much"—whatever that means. It's really impossible to masturbate too much because when your body has had enough it will no longer respond to your efforts to have an orgasm. However, given the strong feelings most people have about the privacy of sex, it is wise to masturbate only in private. Little children don't know this, which partly explains why they get punished for a harmless activity.

I think it will be useful to state some facts about masturbation, just to help remove any fears you or your parents may have. Masturbation is harmless to the body. It does not cause mental illness as some have claimed, (although it can be followed by a damaging sense of guilt and shame in people brought up to fear it); it does not lessen a person's later capacity to enjoy sex in marriage. The stories about its causing pimples, circles under the eyes, weakness, or various diseases are just plain myths and are not to be taken seriously.

Masturbation is a source of sexual pleasure. You get no diseases from it, and nobody ever became pregnant by masturbating. It serves to release sexual tension which otherwise might push people into having sexual intercourse before they are emotionally ready for it or any of its possible consequences. In addition, masturbation can provide an outlet for a person's sexual imagination and daydreaming. Some boys and girls are very worried about the thoughts they have while they masturbate, and at many other times. They should not be, for sexual fantasies of all kinds are common.

Masturbation can help a boy or man learn how to delay his ejaculation and prolong his erection during a period of sexual stimulation. Then later on, when he is ready for intercourse, he will be less likely to ejaculate too soon, before his partner is satisfied. Also, masturbation can help a woman learn how to achieve an orgasm. It is an unhappy fact that many women take years to learn that they can have an orgasm, and some never do. Masturbation can help them to achieve this pleasure earlier, as a part of intercourse or apart from it.

CHAPTER THIRTEEN

Some ways that sex can become a problem

Automobiles, fire, sex—they all have power. Whether their power produces good or bad results depends on how the power is used. Automobiles are a valuable means of transportation, but they become a problem when, largely because of irresponsible use, they kill and injure millions of Americans every year. Fire is essential for cooking, heating, and industry, but it becomes a problem when it destroys houses and factories, burns people, or helps launch the weapons of death. And sex, delightful and productive as it is for carrying on the human race, binding people and families together, and giving great pleasure, can also become a problem in ways that are described below.

Sex Used Selfishly

Perhaps the most common problem of sex is people's misuse of sexual power or attractiveness for their own selfish purposes without consideration of the others involved. I am not talking simply about achieving the intense bodily pleasure that comes from orgasm. It is true that in many ways this is a self-centered pleasure, but in a loving couple each partner will care about the pleasure of the other. I am talking about the husband who insists that his wife have sex with him when she doesn't feel like it; about the girl who looks and acts especially sexy just to tease a boy and then humiliates him by refusing; about the boy who pretends to love a girl in order to win her when all he really intends to do is to make a conquest and build up his own ego; about people who engage in close sexual contact when they know they have a sexually transmitted disease (see Chapter 15); about people who abuse children to get sexual pleasure; about the young couples who openly display their sexual behavior even when they know that it makes their parents or other older people feel uncomfortable or frightened; about the boy or man who hurries a girl or woman into sexual intercourse without troubling to understand her need as a person to feel cared for and loved, and her body's need to be made ready to respond to and enjoy the sexual experience. Sex is good when it is used responsibly, considerately, and understandingly by both partners; it becomes a problem when people use others as objects for their own selfish pleasure.

Sex and Bad Feelings

Sex becomes a problem when, because of the way they were brought up or because of their experiences with sex, people develop bad feelings about it. If boys or girls have been made to believe that sex is evil, that to enjoy bodily pleasures is bad or sinful, then they will feel guilty and unhappy about their sexual desires, and it will probably take them much longer to learn how to have a happy and successful marriage and sexual relationship. A couple who love and care for each other can help each other overcome such bad feelings.

Another bad feeling that many people suffer from is the notion that they aren't good enough sexually. Somehow they have come to believe that sex is a performance, something to be accomplished, and the more the better. Well, if people try to prove something by the number of times they have intercourse, or by the number of people they have it with, they've got the wrong idea. Probably the champion copulators among mammals are guinea pigs, hamsters, rabbits, rats, or mice. So, if you want to prove you're a great mouse or rabbit, try for a large number of copulations. But remember that human beings are different. The real measures of excellence are the qualities of joy, caring, love, and faithfulness that are expressed by sexual activity.

Still another way that people develop bad feelings about sex is from reading too many foolish books and misleading advertisements, listening to too much romantic popular music, and seeing too many TV shows and movies based on fantasy and unrealistic expectations. This may lead them to believe that if their sex life isn't a constant ecstasy, or if they and their partner don't experience an orgasm every time with heavenly bells ringing, there's something wrong with them. Or because they don't resemble magazine models or movie stars, they feel that they can't be desirable and attractive and satisfying to the person they choose to love and who chooses to love them.

With maturity, we can gradually unlearn these feelings of inadequacy by coming to understand that the most important thing is the quality of our relationship with the other person, not the shape of our body or the frequency of our intercourse. There are many people who live loving lives together with sex as an important, but certainly not the only important, part of their lives, and there are those for whom sexual activity is not important at all. These people come in all shapes, sizes, colors, and varieties. But if you expect constant bliss, you are almost certainly going to feel bad about yourself and your sex life.

Adults Who Molest Children

Another problem of sex is the grown man—or, much less often, the grown woman—who approaches young girls and boys and seeks sexual contact with them. This person might be a stranger, but more often he or she is a family relative or someone else the young person knows well. If you know that the possibility of these approaches exists, you will be better prepared to deal with them. You can avoid being alone with such a person. Whether you are a boy or a girl, it is always wise for you to steer away from men or women who approach you in an overfriendly manner or who go out of their way to touch you and try to persuade you in a secret way to be alone with them.

You may have read in the newspaper about a young boy or girl being **molested** by a man. This means that the man has used the young person in an attempt to satisfy his sexual desires, perhaps by exposure of his genitals, perhaps by trying to touch the genitals of the young person. People who do this sort of thing are mentally ill and need help.

If something like this should ever happen to you, you should tell your parents or someone you trust right away, no matter how puzzled or distressed you may feel. Tell exactly what happened; give a plain report. Remember that it was not your fault. If you tell about it, not only will you feel less upset by the experience, but you may make it possible for the person to receive help and be prevented from troubling other young people.

Incest

Incest means intimate sexual relations or sexual intercourse between close relatives, such as father and daughter, mother and son, brother and sister, grandfather and grandchild, uncle and niece. It involves sexual activity that is more serious than that of molesting. Almost every society has strong taboos against incest, and it is considered a crime in every state in the U.S. The reason commonly given for laws against incest is that any child that might result from such sexual intercourse is more likely to suffer from hereditary diseases than is a child resulting from intercourse between a couple who are not close relatives. A much more important reason for condemning incest is that it often means the exploitation of a younger member of a family by an older one in a situation where the younger person feels trapped and finds it difficult to seek help.

It can also upset normal family relationships, making it harder for those involved to establish healthy sexual attachments outside the family and in marriage. A young person who finds himself or herself being forced or tempted into a relationship of incest should seek help at once, from either another member of the family or someone outside.

Rape

Rape is another misuse of sex, and a very serious one. It is sexual intercourse forced by one person upon another, usually by a man upon a woman; so it is really an act of violence using sex as a weapon. Sometimes boys and men are raped, usually by other men, and often in prisons; so sometimes are infants and old people. Rapes are almost always performed by heterosexual men. The rapist may use a gun, a knife, or the threat of physical force to subdue his victim; he may threaten to harm or kill her if she screams or struggles. Rapists are dangerous and mentally sick, and their motives are almost always hostility, aggressiveness, and a desire to harm people, rather than overpowering sexual desire. A rapist no more rapes because he is sexually aroused than an alcoholic drinks because he or she is merely thirsty.

It is important to know that many, probably most rapes are committed not by strangers but by men the females already know. And they are more likely to occur in the woman's home or apartment, which the rapist enters, than outside somewhere.

Another kind of rape is "date rape," when a boy (rarely a girl) forces his partner by any means to have intercourse against her will.

If a woman is threatened with rape, the rapist may not expect resistance, and she may be able to catch him off guard. A sudden loud scream to summon help, a quick act of resistance, and running away in the direction of other people probably are more likely to save her from rape than are attempts to talk or persuade. However, if the rapist threatens her with a weapon and she judges that she is in imminent danger of serious injury, screaming and struggling can be very risky. Then attempted persuasion in the form of calm, strong words to the rapist as a human being, may be the only possibility until the attention of others can be attracted.

Tragic and cruel as rape is, it does not mean the end of the world for the person raped. A woman will never forget the shock of it. She may often feel guilt as well as anger and fear. But she can be helped to get over these feelings and receive the support she needs by talking with someone, especially a skilled counselor who has had experience with rape cases. A doctor can determine whether or not she might be pregnant or have contracted a sexually transmitted disease (see Chapter 15).

A person who has been raped or threatened can help protect others by informing the police without delay. If there is a police investigation, the woman must be prepared to give evidence. Unfortunately, this sometimes involves misguided and embarrassing questions about her personal life. There may even be the suggestion that because she is an attractive female she somehow invited the attack. This is ridiculous. No woman asks to be raped. If a rape victim needs help, or feels victimized by the investigation process, in many communities she or her family can get assistance from a rape crisis center, often listed in the phone book under "Rape."

Language and Sex

Sometimes talking about sex can become a problem. This is partly because many people think of sex as "dirty," and they think that words—especially the short, easy words—and jokes about sex are also dirty. Or it may be because they feel so strongly that sex should be private, even hidden, that they believe it shouldn't be talked about. When you hear people use the expression "four-letter words," they are referring to words like "fuck." This word is slang for "sexual intercourse" and comes from the old Dutch word *fokken,* meaning "to breed," as with cattle. It has been a part of the English language for hundreds of years. The word is objectionable to many people, and any sensitive, intelligent present-day user of English should know this.

Of course there is nothing essentially "dirty" about any word, for a word is merely a symbol for an idea or meaning— the sound of a group of letters. But many words do carry with them strong emotional feelings, especially words having to do with sex, and you should keep this in mind. Otherwise, you may possibly anger and shock people by your language, even though you may not mean to do so, and cause them to condemn you.

An even greater problem than talking too much about sex is not talking at all about it, not being able to communicate with others about it. To enable you to communicate more easily and intelligently about sex is one of the main reasons I wrote this book. If you are in doubt, discuss your questions with close friends or family; tell about your feelings and listen to those of others. (See more about this in Chapter 16, "Sex and Social Life.")

CHAPTER FOURTEEN

Contraception:
preventing unwanted pregnancy

It is possible for a couple who have intercourse regularly to have a child every year, or even more often. In such a case, if the wife married at age twenty and reached menopause (when her ovaries stopped producing eggs) at forty-six, the marriage would produce more than twenty-five children. There are few couples who would have enough money or physical and psychological strength to take good care of such a large family, even if they wanted it. Therefore most married couples practice what is called **family planning.** To do this they use **contraception,** or **birth control.** This means that they decide how many children they can provide for and care for and plan how far apart they wish to space them. Then they limit childbirth according to this plan.

In recent years, most thoughtful people have come to agree that family planning is a necessity. For many families, the arrival of an additional child may be a tragedy. It means another person to feed, clothe, and care for; and food, clothing, and care cost money—often more money than a poor or even a middle-income family can earn. Also, it is sometimes hard on the health of the mother to have another baby, especially too soon after she has had the last one. Some mothers, though, choose to have all of their children in close succession so that they and their husbands will spend a relatively short period of their lives caring for young children.

In addition, the mother, father, and the other children

may all suffer from psychological strains in families that are too large to be cared for adequately and in which over a long period of years there is almost always another infant requiring special attention. It is usually far better if each baby is assured of a welcome because it is planned for and wanted. Then its parents feel they can give it the home, love, and mental stimulation that it needs.

Usually even worse than the birth of an unwanted child to a married couple is the birth of a child to a young couple who are having intercourse but are not married and are not ready to be married. A baby born of unmarried parents is **illegitimate,** meaning "not according to the law or the rules," but this word is seldom used these days because really it is the parents who should be considered illegitimate, not the baby. It is no fault of the baby's. Also, a baby can be well cared for by unmarried parents if they truly love and cherish it and are mature enough to raise it.

Special Problems of Teenage Pregnancy

During the past fifteen years there has been a rapid rise in the number of teenage pregnancies. This has had two results: a large increase in the number of abortions performed on teenage girls (see pages 85–87) and a large increase in babies born to teenage girls, babies whose mothers and fathers are not yet mature adults. Babies born to teenagers quite often suffer from serious problems, largely because the young mothers fail to get good medical care and nutrition and also receive little support from their families or from the fathers of the babies. The babies may be born underweight and undernourished and are more likely to be sickly or to die in infancy. They are more likely to suffer from birth defects or to be mentally retarded. They are more likely to be abused and battered by their parents, who aren't able to cope with parenthood. (It's easy to love a cuddly little newborn baby. It takes a lot more strength to love and nurture a growing child who cries, yells, demands attention, and must be looked after day and night.) Children of teenage parents often have a low opinion of themselves, lack self-respect, and feel they are no good. Also, they often repeat the cycle of their parents, having their own babies at a very young age, and so on—"kids having kids."

And the teenagers themselves who have a baby commonly suffer from serious problems. They may be isolated, lonely, and frustrated. They often drop out of school, and thus only low-paying, low-status jobs are available to them—there's no time for more education and job training. They frequently have to go on welfare. If they decide to get married, their marriages are likely to be unhappy and to end in separation, abandonment, or divorce.

If a teenage girl gets pregnant and decides not to have an abortion, she and her parents should be sure that the girl learns how to care for herself and her unborn baby—that she has good, early **prenatal care**. This should include not only care for the mother and her baby but also training for both the mother and the father in **parenting**: how to be a good parent who can bring up, nurture, and care for babies and young children. Sources of prenatal care and training in parenting can often be found in the telephone book under "Family," "Family Service," "Catholic [or other] Church," "Planned Parenthood," and "School" (many local school districts have programs). One very good booklet on parenting is *Changes: Becoming a Teenage Parent*, available at low cost from Planned Parenthood of Southeast Pennsylvania, 1220 Sansom Street, Philadelphia, PA 19107. Another excellent book is *Parenting, a Guide for Young People* by Sol Gordon and Mina Wollin, published by Sadlier, Inc., 11 Park Place, NY, NY 10007. The U.S. government also provides some good, inexpensive brochures. However, the real solution to the problem of unwanted babies is prevention of pregnancy, either by people not having sexual intercourse or by their using a reliable method of contraception or birth control.

Family Planning and World Population

There is another urgent reason for family planning. Rapidly increasing population has become one of the world's greatest problems. As of 1984, there were more than 4½ billion people on our planet. In less than twenty years the population has increased by about 50 percent. At the present rate of increase, scientists estimate the world's population will be about 7 billion by the year 2000. Before long, the world's resources will not be sufficient to support all the people being born. Indeed, this situation already exists in many countries, especially in Asia, Africa, and Latin America. Therefore humankind must learn how to limit the population to the number of people who can be well taken care of. One result of overpopulation is overwhelming competition, hunger, and disease. Another result is the overuse and pollution of the limited supply of land, minerals, water, and air that are available to us.

Methods of Birth Control

Today, some practice of contraception, or birth control, is legal in every state and accepted by every major religion in the United States. The main discussion concerns the methods of contraception. The Catholic Church officially opposes methods that it considers to be "unnatural" and thus against the will of God. It is important for all people to respect the strong moral feelings of many Catholics on this matter. It is equally important for Catholics to respect the moral feelings of those who favor other methods of contraception. (See "Natural Family Planning," pages 78–80.)

Knowledge of the methods of contraception is part of the information about sex that every person should have. Biologically, *what is essential in preventing the conception of a child is keeping a live sperm cell from joining a live egg cell and fertilizing it.* Here are the contraceptive methods most commonly used:

ABSTINENCE

Abstinence means to abstain from (not to have) sexual intercourse. Some people go through their entire lives abstaining from sexual intercourse, and, obviously, they do not impregnate nor become pregnant. Others abstain from intercourse during the period when the woman is likely to be ovulating. (See "Natural Family Planning," pages 78–80.) Many teenagers, contrary to reports and messages on TV, in the press, and in popular music, have not had sexual intercourse. However, over the past fifteen years, the number of teenagers who do not abstain has increased.

There are a number of reasons why abstinence can be considered the best method of birth control for teenagers. These are given in Chapter 16, "Sex and Social Life." However, for most married couples, sexual sharing is an important part of their relationship. For them abstinence is not a satisfactory method of family planning. (Chapter 16 also discusses ways of enjoying bodily closeness and pleasure without having intercourse and risking pregnancy.)

THE PILL

Birth control pills are taken orally and cause chemical (hormonal) changes in the woman's body that stop her from ovulating. Thus no egg is released to be fertilized. There are many varieties of pills, and the exact way they work is very complicated. However, they are simple to use. One pill a day is taken for three weeks, beginning on the fifth day after menstruation starts, and then the pills are stopped for one week, during which time a vaginal flow like menstruation takes place. The pills are usually sold in special dispensers that help the woman remember to take her pill. Some dispensers contain a pill to be taken every day; the spaces in the dispenser for the no-pill days contain a placebo pill, one that contains no hormones. This makes it even easier never to forget to take the needed pill. Taking a pill for only one day, or a few days, has no contraceptive effect. A girl who gets a few pills from her mother or a friend and then has intercourse is just as likely to get pregnant as one who uses no pill at all. Different pills are prescribed for different women, and no one should ever take a birth control pill that has been prescribed for someone else.

The pills may be used only when prescribed by a doctor, who should explain their possible side effects. For regular users, it is an advantage to obtain a six-month or year's supply. When a woman stops taking her pills, even for a day or two, she may quickly become pregnant if she has sexual intercourse unless she uses another method of contraception.

There is probably no increased risk of cancer from taking the pill. It may, in fact, protect against certain cancers. However, women over thirty-five who take the pill and smoke are somewhat more likely to get heart disease.

INTRAUTERINE DEVICES (IUD)

Intrauterine devices, called **IUDs,** are coils, loops, T's or other shapes, usually made of plastic, any one of which is inserted by a doctor into the flat, triangular cavity of the uterus. By means not yet entirely understood, the IUD either keeps the egg from implanting itself in the wall of the uterus or prevents fertilization of the egg. The IUD has one or two thin plastic threads attached to it that hang down through the cervix so that the woman can feel them with her finger and thus make a regular check to be sure that the IUD has not been expelled.

The advantages of the IUD are its low cost and the simplicity of its use, for once it has been inserted, nothing more needs to be done except for the woman to make an occasional checkup visit to the doctor. It is very reliable, especially when used by women who have had a child and whose uterine cavity is therefore permanently somewhat enlarged and thus less likely to expel the IUD. The IUD has about the same rate of success as the pill.

However, in some instances, particularly in women who have never been pregnant, the IUD may cause pain, cramps, and bleeding, and even infection and blocking of the fallopian tubes. Therefore many doctors do not recommend it, especially for women who have never been pregnant. (See "Pelvic Inflammatory Disease," page 92.)

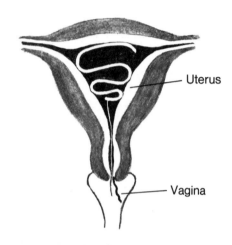

IUD IN PLACE IN UTERUS

DIAPHRAGM

A **diaphragm** is a round rubber cap, usually about 2 to 3 inches in diameter, which the woman places in the vagina to block off the cervix, or neck of the womb, from the main part of the vagina. (It does not block the urethra or have any effect on a woman's urination.) The diaphragm prevents the sperm from entering the cervix, and it is used with a special kind of cream or jelly that kills sperm cells (a **spermicide**). It can be inserted up to two hours before intercourse, and it must be left in for several hours after to make sure that all the sperm are dead. A diaphragm is obtained by prescription only and must be fitted by a doctor, who shows the woman how to insert it. It has no negative side effects since it is not irritating to the body, nor does it introduce any possibly harmful chemicals into a woman's body. To be effective, it must be used exactly according to the doctor's instructions.

CONTRACEPTIVE SPONGE

The **contraceptive sponge** is a sponge made of plastic. It contains sperm-killing chemicals which are released gradually over a period of about twenty-four hours. A woman inserts the sponge into her vagina up against the cervix before she expects to have intercourse, and it must be left in at least 6 hours after intercourse. In some women the sponge causes discomfort and an allergic reaction. Not more than twenty-four hours after insertion, the sponge must be removed (by means of a small loop attached to it) and discarded. Contraceptive sponges are available at drugstores without prescription.

CONDOM

A **condom** is a thin rubber device shaped like the finger of a glove, which is placed over the man's erect penis before intercourse and prevents the sperm from escaping into the vagina. It is often called a "rubber" or a "safe." If the condom is new *and* if the man does not use it while the woman's vagina is still dry *and* if when he puts it on he leaves a small space at the end of the penis to receive the ejaculated semen *and* if he carefully holds the condom in place with his fingers and withdraws his penis before he loses his erection so that no semen will spill into the vagina, then the condom is a very effective means of contraception. Also, there must be no continuation of intercourse without changing condoms.

If condoms are carelessly or inexpertly used, they are not reliable. However, when they are used with care, they are a highly effective means of contraception, especially if the woman also uses a contraceptive foam or jelly. (Condoms must not be used with a petroleum product like Vaseline, which quickly damages the rubber.) Another advantage of the condom and foam is that they help prevent the spread of sexually transmitted diseases (see Chapter 15). Condoms are available at drugstores without prescription.

FOAMS, CREAMS, JELLIES

There are a number of spermicidal foams, creams, and jellies that a woman can place in her vagina before intercourse, which may block or kill the sperm and thus prevent fertilization of the egg. Used alone, however carefully, these are not as effective as the methods described above, but they are much better than nothing. Also, as I have said, they are very good to use with diaphragms and condoms. Foams, creams, and jellies are available at drugstores without prescription.

NATURAL FAMILY PLANNING

Natural family planning (NFP) means methods of birth control—of preventing pregnancy or of choosing when a woman shall become pregnant—based on **fertility awareness.** It is called "natural" because it uses no chemicals nor artificial devices to prevent conception. "Fertility awareness" means learning how to recognize the time when a woman is about to ovulate or has ovulated. If a couple do not wish a pregnancy, they must not have sexual intercourse for several days *before* ovulation (since sperm may remain alive in a woman's body for two to five days after ejaculation) through several days *after* ovulation, when the unfertilized egg disintegrates.

There are four methods of natural family planning:

Cervical mucus method: This method (sometimes called the **Billings Ovulation Method** after the doctors who developed it) is based on the fact that noticeable wet, slippery mucus comes from the cervix for a few days before ovulation. The woman evaluates her cervical mucus by feeling it with her fingers. Wet, slippery mucus signals that she is **fertile** and can become pregnant. (The mucus also facilitates the passage and survival of sperm within the woman's reproductive organs.) After ovulation, the mucus becomes sticky or disappears.

Basal body temperature method (BBT): This method is based on the fact that the temperature of most healthy women rises just after ovulation takes place. Using a special thermometer, a woman takes her temperature each morning when she wakes up and keeps a careful record of it on a chart. Under normal circumstances, her temperature remains elevated until she next menstruates.

Cervical os method: The cervical os is the opening at the entrance to the cervix. Just before a woman ovulates, the os softens (so it feels more like a person's lips than a nose), opens slightly, and moves higher up within the vagina. When a woman notices this as she feels her cervical os with her fingers, she knows that ovulation is approaching. After ovulation the os closes, becomes firm, and returns to its lower position.

Calendar method: The calendar method involves keeping a record on a chart over a period of months of the dates on which a woman's menstrual period occurs and thus estimating the time of her next ovulation. Unlike the other NFP methods, the calendar method depends upon a woman's menstrual cycle being regular. Since many women, and especially teenagers, have irregular menstrual periods, the calendar method (which used to be called the "rhythm" method) is unreliable and is not taught by modern natural family planning practitioners.

If a woman wants to use natural family planning, it is essential that she, preferably with her husband, take a training course from a specialist who teaches exactly how to use the methods correctly. It is also essential that the directions be followed carefully and consistently.

Many couples report that they like NFP because it puts them in touch with each other and with what is going on in their own bodies. They feel that sharing this aspect of their relationship means equality in family planning decisions. Since the methods are considered natural, they are approved by the Catholic Church.

WITHDRAWAL

Withdrawal is an old and commonly used method. It requires the man to withdraw his penis from the woman's vagina just before ejaculation so that the semen is deposited well away from her vagina. The withdrawal method is quite unreliable because the man may not withdraw his penis soon enough. Also, even before ejaculation his penis may secrete a small quantity of fluid containing sperm.

Although withdrawal is better than nothing, a couple who use this method are very likely to create a pregnancy. Further, if the man ejaculates near the vaginal opening, it is very risky and pregnancy may well result.

STERILIZATION

Still another method, used by people who wish never to have any more children, involves **sterilization** of either the man or the woman in a way that prevents fertilization yet does not lessen either one's capacity to enjoy intercourse. In men it is done by means of a minor, easy, and harmless surgical operation. A short section from each vas deferens, the tube that carries the sperm from the testicles, is cut and the remaining ends are tied. Instead of passing along the tube, the sperm are absorbed into the man's body. Thus no sperm are contained in the semen when the man ejaculates. Since the sperm make up only a microscopically small part of the semen, there is not a noticeable reduction in the quantity of semen. The operation is called a **vasectomy.**

Women can be sterilized by having their fallopian tubes

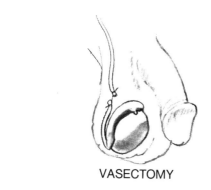

VASECTOMY

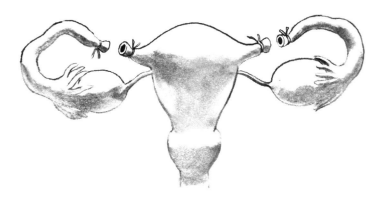

TUBAL LIGATION

STERILIZATION OF MALE (*top*) AND FEMALE (*bottom*)

tied and cut by a surgeon so that egg cells cannot pass from the ovary into the uterus. This operation is called a **tubal ligation.** At present, it is a more difficult operation than a vasectomy and must be done in a hospital, though doctors have developed a technique to do it almost as quickly and simply as a vasectomy. This process is called a **laparoscopy.** A small incision is made in the navel (so that the scar will not be noticeable) and a miniature telescope is inserted, through which the doctor can see the fallopian tubes. The doctor inserts an electric cauterizer to burn out a small section of each tube and to close up the ends so that no eggs or sperm can pass.

Neither a vasectomy nor a tubal ligation interferes with the enjoyment of sexual intercourse; they may actually increase enjoyment because the worry about pregnancy and the need for using any kind of device is gone. Both operations should be considered permanent. Another operation may be performed to undo them, but this has much less than a fifty-fifty chance of succeeding and thus cannot be relied upon. Neither operation is appropriate for young people, who can't predict if they will want to be parents later in their lives.

THE "MORNING-AFTER" PILL

If a woman has intercourse without using any reliable means of contraception, there is one last possibility for avoiding pregnancy. It is called the "morning-after" pill and involves a massive dose of hormones given within a day or two after intercourse. It is thought that this dose prevents implantation of the fertilized egg in the uterus. The dose usually makes the woman very nauseated for a few days, as well as causing headaches, diarrhea, and dizziness, and many doctors don't like to prescribe it. However to the best of our knowledge, it causes no permanent harm.

Other methods of birth control are being investigated by scientists and doctors, who feel, almost without exception, that a low-cost, easy, sure and safe method of preventing unwanted pregnancy and limiting the size of families—and a method that will be acceptable to all—will be beneficial to humankind.

Methods of Contraception That Do Not Work

It is important to emphasize that there is much wrong and dangerous information passed around about birth control methods. Some uninformed people try methods that do not work:

Douches (squirting liquid into the vagina after intercourse): It's too late. Sperm enter the cervix immediately after ejaculation. They cannot be reached by a douche.

Plastic wrap in place of a condom: It tears and allows the sperm to escape.

Urination right after intercourse: The urine passes through the urethra, not the vagina, and so does not affect the sperm. (See the drawing on page 8.)

Using a special position for intercourse: As long as the penis enters (or comes very near) the vagina and semen is ejaculated, fertilization may take place, no matter what position the couple use when they have intercourse.

Having intercourse while the woman is menstruating: A woman can get pregnant from intercourse during her menstrual period.

Having intercourse while the woman is nursing her baby: If she has intercourse, a woman can get pregnant whether she is nursing or not, although the likelihood is reduced.

Having intercourse the first time: A woman can get pregnant even though she has never had intercourse before.

Sources of Help

Fortunately, it is now possible in most cities and in many rural areas for people to receive expert advice on contraception and to obtain the birth control products they need. Organizations such as Planned Parenthood and most public health and medical centers provide these services confidentially, at no cost if the user cannot pay. The Catholic Church and other churches also provide such services. No one of any age should be afraid or embarrassed to ask for information about birth control. For any person who is going to have sexual intercourse and does not want to have and care for a child, it is a must.

It is also advisable in almost every case for young people who are considering having sexual intercourse to talk the matter over with their parents, including methods of birth control. This may seem difficult in some families, but it almost always is worth the effort.

Reliability of Methods

Quite a lot of research has been done on the reliability of the different methods of contraception. A great deal depends on how intelligently and conscientiously the couple uses the method selected, and on how carefully they were taught how to use it. There is usually a great difference between theoretical effectiveness (if the method were used perfectly) and actual-use effectiveness (taking into account the mistakes people make, including forgetting). Out of any 100 women having intercourse regularly over a period of a year, how many will become pregnant? Here are the estimates of actual-use effectiveness:

Using no contraceptive at all	90 would be pregnant
Using withdrawal	20–25 would be pregnant
Using natural family planning	2–30 would be pregnant (research statistics vary)
Using a sponge	17 would be pregnant
Using a recommended foam, cream, or jelly*	15 would be pregnant
Using a diaphragm with sperm-killing cream or jelly	10 would be pregnant
Using a condom*	10 would be pregnant

Using an IUD	4 would be pregnant
Using the pill	2 would be pregnant
Being sterilized	almost none would be pregnant

Very often when young people are considering having sexual intercourse and using birth control, they find it difficult to act in a calm and intelligent manner. They are embarrassed, anxious (even afraid), awkward, forgetful, and careless, especially if they don't have a good sense of self-respect and are confused by the negative things they have been taught about touching and talking about the genital parts of the body. To be effective users of birth control methods, they must:

- *learn* the methods;
- *remember* the methods;
- *acknowledge* in advance that they are likely to be sexually active;
- *obtain* the method they expect to use;
- *discuss* the method with their partner;
- *use* the method.

Abortion

When a couple does not use contraception or if contraception fails and the woman becomes pregnant, she will have to decide what to do. One of the possibilities is **abortion**—that is, having the embryo removed by a simple surgical procedure. When done early in pregnancy by a qualified physician in a hospital or specially equipped clinic, abortions are quite safe—safer, for example, than childbirth. In the first trimester (three months) of pregnancy, they are done on an outpatient basis;

---

*Recent studies show that condoms and foam, correctly and carefully used together, are a very effective method of contraception. They have the advantages, too, of involving both the male and the female in the contraceptive activity and in protecting against sexually transmitted diseases.

there is no need to stay overnight at a hospital or clinic. However, no abortion is a minor matter, and abortions later in pregnancy present a greater chance of surgical complications and often involve an overnight stay in the hospital. If the abortion is performed before the twelfth week of pregnancy, the doctor may use a suction machine which removes the embryo and other products of conception. About 90 percent of the abortions performed in the United States are done at some time during the first twelve weeks. Obviously, the sooner a girl or woman reports an overdue menstrual period to her doctor or to a clinic, the better.

If abortions are done in secret or illegally, it is almost impossible to check on the qualifications of the doctor or the adequacy of the equipment and procedures. In such cases, abortions may be dangerous and can permanently injure or even kill a woman.

In 1973, the U.S. Supreme Court ruled that it is the right of any woman, in consultation only with her doctor, to have an abortion performed within the first trimester of pregnancy and that state laws interfering with this right are unconstitutional. For abortions after the first trimester, states are allowed to pass laws that are related to protecting the life or health of the mother. And for abortions during the last three months of pregnancy, when the fetus may be **viable** (that is, if it is born prematurely and given proper special care, it could live), states are allowed to pass laws taking into consideration the welfare of the fetus as well as that of the mother.

There are many people who feel that it is wrong to terminate even the beginnings of human life. They feel so strongly about this that they even say that abortion is murder. One of the moral questions a person has to decide is this: Is there a difference between removing an embryo or a fetus, which is growing toward being a person, and killing an existing person, born and actually living out in the world? Two other questions are: Does a woman have the right to choose for herself between giving birth and having an abortion? Do others have the right to make that decision for her? The Supreme Court's ruling stated that the U.S. Constitution considers a being to be a person only after he or she is born and said that we don't know enough at present to "resolve the difficult question of when life begins."

In any case, when a girl or woman is considering an abortion, it is important that she receive help and advice from a trained and sympathetic counselor as to whether she should continue or terminate her pregnancy. Sometimes the decision, either way, may affect her emotionally more deeply than she expected it would, especially if the abortion is performed after the first trimester, and she will need help in dealing with these effects. The counselor can also see that she gets birth control advice so that she will not have another unwanted pregnancy.

Abortion is certainly a very poor method of birth control. Is it better than allowing a child unwanted by its own mother and father to be born into a family, or to a mother without a family, where the chances of receiving good physical care and sufficient love support may be slim? For many people, this is not an easy question to answer.

CHAPTER FIFTEEN

STD: Sexually transmitted disease (VD)

Another problem of sex is **sexually transmitted disease,** often called **venereal disease** (VD). (The word "venereal" means "having to do with sexual intercourse" and comes from Venus, the name of the Roman goddess of love.) STDs are spread by sexual intercourse and by other intimate sexual activity, such as heavy petting, during which warm, moist parts of people's bodies come in contact—parts like the vulva, vagina, penis, mouth, and rectum. In the late 1960s, after a long period of decline, the frequency of STDs began to increase rapidly in the United States, especially among teenagers, and it is very important for anyone who is or may become sexually active to know about them.

There are about a dozen sexually transmitted diseases that are quite common—some dangerous, some not. Sometimes they come in combinations, so it is not easy to diagnose them. For many STDs the treatment is simple and short, but some of the diseases linger or return, and their treatment is not so simple. There's not space in this book to explain all of the diseases, nor does one need to understand them all. The most important thing for people to know is the main symptoms of STD and how to get diagnosed and treated by a doctor or by a clinic specializing in STD treatment. Both the person with the symptoms *and* that person's sexual partner or partners should be diagnosed and treated.

The Main STDs

The five main sexually transmitted diseases are **gonorrhea, trichomonas, herpes, nongonococcal urethritis** (**NGU**), and **syphilis.** Some of them may lead to a serious condition in women called **pelvic inflammatory disease** (**PID**). We'll discuss PID later.

GONORRHEA

Commonly called "the clap," "the drip," or "a dose," gonorrhea seldom causes death, but if not treated promptly it can lead to pregnancy in the fallopian tubes, sterility, and crippling arthritis. The disease is caused by the **gonococcus** germ, which can live only in warm, moist places, such as inside the human body, and it usually gets its start inside the vagina or the penis and the rest of the reproductive tract. Gonorrhea is epidemic throughout the world today, being the most commonly reported infectious disease in the United States, with about one million new cases occurring each year.

In most cases it is easy for a man to know he has gonorrhea, because a few days after he has become infected he will notice a painful burning when he urinates and pus will drip from his penis. On the other hand, a woman can carry the germs without having any symptoms because the germs live and multiply around her cervix, where the tissue has less feeling than in the urethra and where no urine, with its acid content, can cause burning as it passes over the area. Therefore a special test is necessary to detect gonorrhea in women. If a man knows he has contracted gonorrhea, he should at once tell any woman with whom he has had sexual intercourse, so that she may be examined immediately and treated if need be. If she is infected and not treated, the disease can seriously damage her body by leading to pelvic inflammation disease (see page 92), and she may unknowingly transmit it to other sexual partners.

The treatment is simple: usually one dose of penicillin or other antibiotic is sufficient. This will nearly always cure a person, but it will not prevent him or her from getting the disease again. There is no immunity. Also, new strains of gonorrhea, which resist treatment by penicillin, are developing throughout the world, including the United States. Thus the time may be near when treatment and cure become much more difficult and expensive.

If gonorrhea is not treated, the germs can spread throughout the body, damaging the sex organs and the joints. It can cause crippling arthritis. Also, when a person's body attempts to repair the damage done by gonorrhea, it may cause scar tissue to block the sperm tubes and tubules in a man, or the fallopian tubes in a woman, preventing the sperm or the egg from getting through. In this way, gonorrhea is a major cause of **sterility,** the inability to have children, in men and women.

Also, and even more seriously, it can cause partial blockage of the fallopian tubes. This reduced opening may be large enough to allow the tiny sperm to pass through and fertilize the egg, but too small to allow the fertilized egg to move by the blockage and into the uterus. Therefore the egg stops in the tube and continues to grow there. This is called a **tubal pregnancy** and is a very painful condition that can endanger the life of the mother. Usually surgery is required to remove the embryo and, if possible, repair the tube.

If a woman with gonorrhea gives birth, her baby may catch the disease as it passes through the birth canal. The eyes especially may be infected and the baby could go blind. This is why all states require that the eyes of all newborn children be treated with a chemical or an antibiotic medicine.

TRICHOMONAS (OR TRICHOMONIASIS)

This disease, even more common than gonorrhea, is often called "trich." It is caused by a single-cell germ, which can live for several hours outside the body. Thus, while you usually can get trichomonas from sexual activity, you can also get it from objects if they are moist and warm and have recently been used by an infected person. In women, the symptoms of the disease are a gray, smelly discharge from the vagina and itching of the genitals. In men there are no definite symptoms, but men transmit the disease. It can be easily cured by Flagyl, prescribed by a doctor for both sexual partners. However, this drug can cause gene mutations and must never be used by pregnant women.

HERPES (GENITAL HERPES)

Herpes of the genitals, caused by herpes simplex virus type 2 (often called just herpes simplex), is one of the fastest growing sexually transmitted diseases in the U.S. today. It is caused by a virus similar to the one that commonly causes cold sores in and around the mouth, herpes type 1. Because it is incurable, genital herpes is more serious than gonorrhea. Nobody knows for sure how many cases there are because doctors and clinics are not required to report the disease to public health authorities. Its symptoms are painful shallow open sores (ulcers) that look like chickenpox, usually accompanied by fever and sometimes by painful urination. Herpes heals itself in about ten days, but in many cases it comes back without re-exposure to an infected person, and it can go on for years. It is passed to others by people with active herpes sores. People should be very careful, therefore, not to kiss, pet, or have any intimate sexual contact with a person who has visible herpes sores on the genitals. As with trichomonas, you can also get herpes from moist, warm objects if they have been recently used by a person with an active case.

If a woman with active herpes gives birth, she can transmit the disease to her baby, causing it to have serious problems. Therefore, the baby should be delivered by *cesarean section*. Doctors are working hard to find a cure for genital herpes, but no totally effective treatment is yet available.

NONGONOCOCCAL URETHRITIS (NGU)

This disease is an inflammation of the urethra. It is probably more common than gonorrhea. The organism causing most cases of NGU is called **chlamydia**. In men NGU causes painful urination, but not as severe as with gonorrhea. In women it also causes painful urination, and there are usually less definite symptoms, such as discharges from the vagina, pelvic aches, and general fatigue. There are a number of causes of NGU other than chlamydia, and the disease can come back. If untreated in women, NGU can lead to pelvic inflammatory disease (PID). Medicine for GNU must be taken for a whole week. Otherwise, it might not cure the disease.

PELVIC INFLAMMATORY DISEASE (PID)

If gonorrhea and NGU are not promptly detected and treated, the bacteria that cause these diseases may spread to a woman's uterus and fallopian tubes and cause **pelvic inflammatory disease** (PID). If the tubes are blocked by the PID infection and scars, the result is sterility (the inability to have children). If the tubes are only partially blocked, tubal pregnancy may result (see "Gonorrhea," above).

The symptoms of PID are severe abdominal pain, fever, and tenderness of the pelvic organs. PID can usually be treated with antibiotic medicine over a seven-day period, but hospitalization is often required. If the medicine does not work, surgery may be necessary. It is most important that PID be diagnosed and treated promptly. If it is not, it may threaten a woman's life. A woman's sexual partner must also be treated so that she will not be reinfected.*

SYPHILIS

Syphilis is caused by little corkscrew-shaped organisms called

---

*Studies show that women who use an intrauterine device (see page 75) are more likely to get pelvic inflammatory disease than those who do not. Therefore IUD users should be alert for PID symptoms.

spirochetes, which circulate in the bloodstream and get deep into the tissues of the body, where they may lie inactive for years. This disease, directly or indirectly, kills hundreds, perhaps thousands, of men and women each year and also causes blindness, heart disease, mental illness, and many other ailments. Syphilis appears in many forms and stages and can cause very painful suffering. It can be passed on to an unborn child through a mother who has not been adequately treated. About 50,000 new cases of syphilis occur each year in the United States.

Fortunately, as soon as it is discovered the disease can be treated quite easily with large doses of penicillin or other antibiotics. There are reliable blood tests for syphilis, which many states require of a man and a woman before they are permitted to marry.

The first symptoms of syphilis are usually slight or similar to those of several other diseases. The most common and definite symptom is a hard, dime-sized, painless, moist sore called a **chancre.** It usually appears, from ten days to three months after exposure, at the place where the spirochetes entered the body: in the man usually on or around the penis, and in the woman on the vulva or deep within the vagina, where it cannot be seen. After a time varying from a few days to a month, the chancre disappears without any treatment, but this does not mean the syphilis has disappeared. It has merely "gone underground." In its second stage, the germs spread through the bloodstream causing several signs and symptoms, a common one being a non-itching rash most often including the palms and soles of the feet.

Syphilis can be passed on from an infected mother to her unborn baby. If the mother is not treated, the baby may very likely be born with the disease, which can lead to blindness, damage to many organs (including the brain), and death. If a pregnant woman is treated and cured, the baby will also be cured, but the treatment cannot undo any damage caused to the baby before treatment.

In 1981 a new and deadly STD was first reported in the United States: **AIDS (Acquired Immune Deficiency Syndrome)**. The disease is transmitted by intimate sexual contact with infected persons or by blood-to-blood contact with an infected person. It causes its victims to lose their immunity—their natural defenses against disease. Thus they die from various infectious diseases, most commonly a kind of pneumonia caused by a parasite, or from a rare kind of cancer of the blood vessels. The symptoms of AIDS are fever, sweats, coughing, swollen glands, diarrhea, and unexplained weight loss. But many people have AIDS without symptoms.

The groups of people most likely to become AIDS victims are homosexual and bisexual men who have many sex partners; abusers of drugs that are injected by needles, especially when they share the same needle; Haitians who have recently entered the U.S.; and people who have a blood disease called hemophilia.

The death rate among AIDS victims is about 60 percent, and may grow since there is as yet no known cure for the disease. Already, health authorities have identified a special virus that causes AIDS and are spending millions of dollars to try to find a cure.

Because of the very high death rate and the likelihood that the disease will spread to other groups and larger numbers of people, AIDS is a major national health threat and will continue to be one until a cure is found, tested, and made available.

Some Annoying Discomforts

There are several other diseases and discomforts of the genitals from which women sometimes suffer, sometimes sexually transmitted, sometimes not. There are so-called **yeast infections** and other vaginal infections, which cause itching and burning. There are also **urinary infections,** which arise because the woman's opening for urine is right next to the vagina and therefore subject to infection. These may cause painful urination and other painful symptoms. Also, both men and women may be afflicted with **crabs,** a kind of lice that gets into the pubic hair and causes itching. Crab lice are passed from one person to another during close physical contact.

If you think you may be infected with any of these diseases, or if you have any unusual symptoms in your genital area, see a doctor or go to a clinic at once for testing and any needed treatment.

Prevention, Treatment, and Cure of STD

If a couple have been examined by a doctor to make sure that neither one is infected with an STD, and if thereafter they have intercourse or close sexual contact only with each other, they need not worry about STD. The people most likely to get STD are those who are sexually active with many partners. If someone you do not know well is willing to have intercourse or other physically intimate sexual contact with you, quite likely that person has had intercourse and sexual contact with other people too, and your chances of getting STD may be pretty high. You should remember that usually it is almost impossible to tell by a person's appearance whether he or she has STD, and if the person is selfish or not caring, he or she may not tell you about such an infection.

One encouraging thing about most STDs (except herpes and AIDS) is that they are quite easy to treat and cure. Therefore, no matter what, if you have any reason to believe you have been exposed to STD infection, you should go *at once* to a public health clinic or to your own doctor for tests. You should be sure to tell the doctor that you think you may have been exposed to STD and ask for tests. If you do not ask, the doctor may not do the necessary tests. You need not feel embarrassed, for such tests and any needed treatment are kept confidential. Don't forget, STDs are diseases, not crimes! If you have a sexually transmitted disease, it is important, too, that any person with whom you have had sexual contact also be tested and treated. In that way they will not get the complications of STD nor will they spread the infection to others.

If you need help in finding a public health clinic near you where you can be tested and, if necessary, treated without cost, or if you have any questions about STD, call the VD (or STD) national hotline, toll-free, at 1-800-227-8922 (1-800-982-5883 in California), 11:00 A.M. to 11:00 P.M. Eastern time, 8:00 A.M. to 8:00 P.M. Pacific time. Your call is confidential. No one asks for your name.

STD Essentials

· If you have any of the following symptoms, you may have an STD:

FEMALES

Gray, smelly discharge from vagina

Unusual quantity of thick or "cheesy" discharge from vagina

Unusual bleeding from vagina

Severe stomach cramps, not connected with menstruation

Painful intercourse

MALES

Milky or yellow discharge from penis

Soreness inside penis

BOTH SEXES

Burning sensation while urinating

Irritation of rectum and pus-covered feces (bowel movement)

Intense itching of genitals

Painless sore on or near vagina or penis

Painful sores or blisters on or near genitals

Small pink growths on genitals

Painless rash on hands, feet, or entire body

• If you have had intimate sexual contact with someone who has STD (or VD), you may contract the STD even though you have no symptoms.

• If any of these symptoms appear, or if there has been the possibility of exposure to STD, don't wait. Go as soon as possible to a doctor or STD (VD) clinic for testing and, if necessary, treatment. Follow their instructions exactly and fully. Testing and treatment at a public health clinic are free.

• For confidential information, call the VD National Hotline (1-800-227-8922; in California, 1-800-982-5883), or look under "Health" or "VD" in the telephone book. They will give advice and the address of the nearest clinic. They do not even ask for your name.

• If symptoms of STD have been detected, it must be made known to any sexual partners so that all involved may be properly treated.

• There are no vaccines or shots that can prevent STD. There is also no such thing as immunity to STD. It may recur again and again with repeated sexual contact with an infected person.

• Intimate sexual contact with many partners, especially with any person one does not know well, greatly increases the chances of contracting STD.

• You should not try to treat yourself. It can be dangerous. STDs change; conditions change; treatments change. Each case can be different. Therefore special up-to-date medical knowledge is needed.

CHAPTER SIXTEEN

Sex and social life

We human beings are social animals. We relate to one another in thousands of different ways, some ways that are loving and caring, some that are hateful and selfish. We can help one another and enrich one another's lives, or we can exploit (use) one another and put one another down.

One part of being a social animal is *communication*. Some people are much better at it than others, and probably all of us could learn to communicate more easily and fully than we do. One of the ways we share our thoughts and feelings is with what is called body language: through our facial expressions, our gestures, our ways of sitting, standing, and moving, and the ways we touch or do not touch each other. We also communicate through words, by what we say and how we say it. Unlike most other animals, whose ways of communication are programmed into them by instinct, we human beings *learn* to communicate. We start learning almost as soon as we are born, and we go right on learning throughout our lives. In those parts of our lives that involve sex and sexual feelings, communication is most important, but for many people it is very difficult. Many couples may have lived together for years, yet have never talked directly and openly about sex and about their sexual feelings toward each other. And there are teenagers who are having a sexual relationship and yet are too embarrassed even to mention birth control to each other, or to talk about their feelings. Of course many couples do develop subtle ways, by touching and by gestures and facial expressions, to communicate with each other without words—again, this is body language. Also, there are couples who are happily married and do very little communicating of any sort about sex. But it is certainly true that many couples would be happier together if they had learned how to communicate openly with each other about their sexuality and their feelings.

There is no way to separate sexual life from the other parts of life, although some people try to. Indeed, this book, which talks mainly about sex, may seem to make such a separation. But sex and sexuality *are* a part of life, a part to accept and live with. Sex is not something from outside that comes in, takes over our bodies temporarily, and then flies off. Some people, however, do see sex in such a way, and they may use this as an explanation, or even an excuse, for sexual actions that are damaging: "I really didn't want intercourse; the feelings just came and overwhelmed me." This attitude is a cop-out from responsibility. True, we cannot deny our feelings; they exist and influence us. We may feel strongly attracted to another person and even wish to have sexual contact with that person. Or we may feel hostile and hateful toward another person. But if we are thoughtful and responsible, we can control our actions. Feeling like having sex doesn't mean that we actually must perform the action. Feeling hostile toward a person doesn't mean that we must actually hit or harm that person. The distinction between feelings and actions is important, in sex and in all the rest of life.

A fact that enriches our social lives is that there are two sexes, male and female. In Chapter 10 you read about differences between men and women, how some of them are inborn and inevitable, but how in many ways we learn to be "masculine" and "feminine," and how it is possible for us today to be much more free to develop into the sort of people we want to be, rather than being so limited by traditional sex roles. We can enjoy relating to each other as women and as men, but also, and even more important, as human beings who share so much in common. The sexual part of a relationship, whether it involves sexual activity or only the expression of ourselves as boys and girls and men and women, can add delight and pleasure that might be missing if there were only one sex.

Sex, then, cannot be separated from the rest of life, but still there are some special things to be said about the pleasures and problems of love and sex as a part of life. One of the problems of sex that we human beings have and animals don't have can be stated quite simply: boys and girls reach puberty (when so many of them begin to have increasingly strong sexual desires) before they are mature enough to enter into a full and satisfying sexual relationship, to marry, or to establish a family and raise children. There is a period of eight to ten years or even longer when the sex urge may be strong but there is no way to satisfy it that is entirely acceptable to all parts of our society.

Some people are concerned that they might not be able to have a good sex life later on if they do not use their sex organs for a number of years. They ask if these organs dry up or grow weak with disuse, just as muscles grow weak if they are not exercised. The answer is "No." Sex organs and muscles are quite different. Most people who have no intercourse until they marry find that their sexual power is strong and adequate in marriage. They can learn how to enjoy their sexuality together more and more. The "first time" is seldom the universe-shaking experience of ecstasy that the sexual messages of our society tell us it is.

The decisions that people make about sexuality will differ with different individuals. The decisions will depend upon the beliefs and teaching each person has been exposed to and how each has reacted to them, as well as the social situations they are in and the values and convictions they develop. Few people ever find final answers for questions as complicated as those relating to sexual behavior. Most of us will go on searching and questioning and learning all of our lives. And it is most likely that we are not going to be willing to behave in certain ways just because we are told to. We will put together the information we have, the values we hold, our idea of the sort of person we want to be, and the things we have been taught—and then decide for ourselves. *If we are responsible, mature people, our decisions will be made in the light of our knowledge of all of the consequences of what we do, consequences good and bad, present and future, for us and for others.*

If the consequences of the actions are likely to be good for all the people involved—for self, partner, family, community—both now and in the future, then perhaps we can say that the actions are *moral*. If they are not good, and especially if the person performing the actions knows that they are not and does them anyway, then they surely are *immoral*. You can see that there is nothing easy about these definitions of "moral" and "immoral." That is why it is such a good idea to talk over your questions about sexual behavior, and all other important kinds of behavior, with people your own age and also with those who have had more life experience than you have and whose wisdom and judgment you respect.

One thing is sure: People's degree of sexual readiness changes as they grow toward maturity. Twelve- to fourteen-year-olds are vastly different from, say, seventeen- to nineteen-year-olds, as they in turn are different from adults. As for how much sexual experience is right at what age, there are probably nearly as many opinions as there are thinking people. Here are two opinions, expressed in class by eighth-grade students of mine, which show the differences there can be even among people the same age. They could have been said by much older people.

One said: "I think sex is recreation, and it should be enjoyed just like any other recreation. Sex gives big physical pleasure and can help two people communicate deeply with each other. If a girl and a boy know what they are doing—I mean, if they take proper precautions to avoid having a baby, and if they are alert to the dangers of VD—then why shouldn't they have sex?

"I don't think they even have to be in love. As long as they both want to do it, they should go ahead and have sex pleasure. It's natural. After all, girls and boys talk together, they dance together, they play together, and all sorts of things like that. Why shouldn't they have sexual intercourse together?"

The other said: "I think the basis for our society is families. And the center of the family is a married couple who ought to love each other. The couple make a home based on their relationship, and this home brings love and security to them and their children.

"A great part of the husband and wife's relationship is sex—not all, but a big part. Having sex helps to keep them close and loyal to each other. There's something absolutely special about having sex, I think, even though I haven't had it yet. I'm not going to have it until I get married, and then I'm only going to have it with my wife.

"I'm not saying that you shouldn't make out some before you're married. Maybe that's O.K., if you like each other and it would help you get to know each other. But sexual intercourse—that should be saved for marriage."

These two students express two contrasting points of view very well, I think. You may agree with one or the other, or partly with each, and your views may well change as you mature and grow older.

Certainly it is natural for boys and girls to be interested in each other and to be interested in sex. If they get to know each other well, they can learn to understand and appreciate their differences and likenesses, and this is excellent preparation for the future and for choosing a husband or wife if they decide they want to marry. When you think about marriage, it's important to remember that you will marry not a body but a *person*—a complex human being with a background of life experience different from yours. The person's body will be important, but not nearly so important in the long run as his or her personality and character.

There is certainly no point in hurrying boy-girl relationships along faster than you desire. People in their early teens are really not yet ready for an intense relationship with a member of the opposite sex. As a matter of fact, a good many boys between the ages of ten and thirteen or even older find girls quite undesirable, even if they are very curious about them. And many girls in the same age group find their boy classmates to be loud, awkward, childish, and generally repulsive. That's all right; both are likely to change in a few years.

However, it is a good idea for boys and girls to have opportunities to get to know each other socially, if they want to. There is a lot of room for friendships between boys and girls in their teens (but no reason for concern if such friendship doesn't develop). There is much pleasure to be had from informal get-togethers such as parties, dances, and picnics.

It is a rare seventh- or eighth-grader who is ready to go steady. A boy and girl who do so at this age may have a pretty dreary and limited life after the first excitement of it. The teens is a good period of life for getting to know many people of both sexes and to know them in many different ways.

In typical classes of twelve- or fourteen-year-olds there are usually a few boys and girls who get all steamed up about parties and dances, about cliques, about who is most popular and who likes whom. They—especially the girls—seem to be afraid that if they don't start being popular right away and don't become active socially as soon as possible, or in with the most "in" group, they may never have a chance. There is no question that their fears are real for them, but they are not based on fact. I've known many, many boys and girls who were miserable because they weren't making it socially in junior high school, who in later grades or in college and in their jobs became popular and enjoyed real social success.

Most people would agree that the true measure of success is not the number of friendships one has but the quality of those friendships.

Many teenagers can even benefit from learning what it is like to be hurt by not enjoying immediate popularity, by having to work to achieve social success. Such experience can teach boys and girls to understand the feelings of others, to be considerate of others, and to do their best to please, support, and help them. In this way they learn that a lasting relationship between people has to be built on more than just physical attractiveness and a good line of conversation. Probably the most important parts of a relationship are common interests and mutual consideration.

In my experience in schools I have often been saddened, and sometimes angered, by the cruel way that some boys and girls make fun of classmates whom they consider different from themselves. Often this ridicule, which includes name-calling, is directed against boys whose physical development is slower than that of most of their classmates or who are not particularly interested in sports, vigorous physical activity, and the sorts of behavior that are too easily labeled "male." Or it is against girls who act like "tomboys," enjoy strenuous sports, and don't like cooking and sewing and pastimes that we label "female." It is wrong, both factually and morally, to take part in such activities, even though they may not be intended to be cruel. It is wrong factually because it assumes that any boy or girl who is not "all boy" or "all girl" is probably going to turn out to be a homosexual, which simply is not so. We usually cannot tell who is gay and who straight, even though the orientation is established early in life, possibly even before birth, and it is not a matter of choice. Labeling people with put-down terms is wrong morally because it is cruel and makes people feel bad about themselves. Also, it assumes that there is only one right way to turn out, that being gay is bad. Look again at Chapter 11, and think again about all this.

It is not easy for most of us to be considerate of the feelings, preferences, and personalities of other people all of the time, especially of people we see as different from ourselves, but it is a sign of maturity to show such consideration and to accept people as they are.

Some Big Questions about Sexual Contacts

I want to say a few words about **necking** and **petting.** Necking is generally understood to include putting your arms around a person's neck or waist, holding hands, sitting close or cheek to cheek, and light kissing. It is a way of expressing your affection for that person, but it does not involve trying to arouse him or her to readiness for sexual intercourse. Petting goes much further and involves deep kissing and caressing the most sensitive parts of the body, such as the breasts or genitals. Petting is the kind of lovemaking that makes a couple ready for intercourse. The term **making out** can refer to either necking or petting. (Many young people refer to "bases," as in baseball, when they talk about physical intimacy. First base is kissing; second base is petting above the waist; third base is petting below the waist; and a home run is "going all the way." These may be convenient terms, but they are not good to use if they promote the idea that sex is just a game and the winner is the one who goes as far as possible.)

It's natural and healthy for people to feel like expressing their affection for other people by touching them. It is a delightful fact that babies and little children crave and need lots of physical love from their parents or those who care for them, and you have probably many times in the past enjoyed a good hug and kiss from your mother or father—and other relatives, too. There can be a similar sort of enjoyment and warmth in physical contact with a member of the other sex who is near your age. Even so, there are some very important things to keep in mind concerning such physical contact, particularly for people in their teens:

Kissing and caressing can bring great pleasure, closeness,

and good feelings; but they may also lead to difficulty. Some boys quickly become so aroused sexually that they lose their willingness to control themselves, and a girl may have difficulty in controlling them. It is also just as possible for some girls to become so involved that they too lose the will to stop. In other words, if you have not decided for yourself, and *in advance of a petting experience*, where you are going to stop, or even whether you are going to start, you may find yourself involved in situations where your physical feelings overwhelm you. You may find yourself engaging in sexual intercourse when you would not have chosen to if you had thought about it. When that happens and you are unprepared, both emotionally and with contraceptives, the long-term results may be tragic: unwanted pregnancy, a sexually transmitted disease, feeling bad about yourself, getting a reputation as a "slut" if the boy tells about it, being "blackmailed" into more unwanted sex.

To avoid such problems, it is important that people think about and discuss their feelings and possible actions. People should try to be sure they understand how the other person is feeling and to explain how they themselves are feeling.

A fact to remember about heavy petting and becoming too sexually aroused is that it is possible—although it is rather rare—for a girl to become pregnant even though she has an intact hymen and has never had intercourse. There is always the natural opening in the hymen through which menstruation flows, and if, in the course of heavy petting, the boy ejaculates near this opening, sperm can make their way into the vagina even though actual intercourse has not taken place. It is because sperm are such active swimmers that they may cause a pregnancy in a girl who is technically still a virgin. It is an unforgivable risk to take.

You should also be aware of the possibility that some boys and girls may try to use a person of the other sex, or sometimes of the same sex, in order to satisfy only their own needs—their need to feel important, their need to feel that they have made it or "scored" and that they are keeping up with their friends or competitors, their need to have something to boast about, or the physical need they feel for a sexual outlet, if they don't accept masturbation. People who don't feel very good about themselves, who don't have much self-respect (respect for themselves as worthy human beings), are apt to act this way. They may think, without even being aware of it, "If I can score, I'll prove I'm really something." In reality it doesn't prove a thing about their worth as a human being. All it shows is that they can have sexual intercourse, something that is true of almost anybody. Merely "having it" is not an accomplishment. "Having it" at the expense of someone else's feelings only shows selfishness and irresponsibility.

People whose feelings of insecurity give them trouble, or who are selfish, may become quite persuasive in trying to persuade or tease a partner into having sexual intercourse. They may pretend to be in love, or even fool themselves into believing that they are in love; they may threaten to cut off a relationship unless their partner has intercourse with them; they may try to make the partner feel small or immature or afraid of not going along; or they may say, in effect, "If you love me, you will prove it by having sex with me."

Saying No to Sexual Intercourse

It is important to learn how to say no to someone who tries to pressure you into having sexual intercourse. Of course, among the realities to keep in mind are the bad results of teenage pregnancy. You read about them on pages 71–72. But even if you know all about birth control and can be almost certain not to become pregnant or to impregnate, there may be other very good reasons for saying no:

• You're just not ready.

• You want to save sexual intercourse for total commitment and marriage.

• You have other overriding interests: getting to know

people on the basis of friendship, not sex; preparing, planning, and setting goals for education, for a job, for a career.

• You reject the idea that, somehow, having intercourse will cure loneliness and unhappiness and make you or your partner feel loved or supported. (By itself, sexual intercourse won't do this.)

• You reject the idea that intercourse will help make you popular. It won't, and if you do it casually with many people it may cause you to lose respect and friendships. A young person said to me recently, "Sex has spoiled some good friendships." If you decide not to have intercourse, and you explain why with confidence and conviction, you probably will stay popular, not lose your boyfriend or girlfriend, and be considered perfectly regular by your friends. If the nature of the crowd you go with means that you do lose a boyfriend or girlfriend or are seen as a square by your group, you may need to consider again what kind of friends you want. I know that this is very hard to do. Friends are very important. Peer pressure is very strong. But there are times, tough as it may be, when you need to try to be even stronger.

• You reject the idea that having intercourse will somehow prove that you are now independent, especially of your parents. Actually, it proves no such thing, even though being independent of parents and learning to stand on your own feet are important goals of adolescence. Sex isn't the way to do it.

• You reject the idea that somehow "the first time" will give you the tremendous feelings of fireworks, excitement, and ecstasy that are so often suggested by TV, records, movies, magazines, and advertising. In fact, "the first time" is usually reported by both sides as a real let-down. "You mean that's it?" many young people say or feel after intercourse that is not a part of a deep, loving relationship.

• You reject the idea that "everybody's doing it." In fact, *not* everybody's doing it.

Many of these are often very difficult, uncomfortable

matters to deal with, but they are worth your best thinking and worth talking over with some other people you trust and who have had more experience than you—your parents, a relative, a teacher, a counselor, a neighbor.

Besides the lines "You would if you loved me" and "Everybody's doing it," there are others worth knowing about and preparing for in advance:

"Don't worry; you won't get pregnant."

"If you get pregnant, I'll marry you."

"But I love you!"

"If you don't, I won't love you anymore."

"I can't stop now, I just can't!"

How Will You Know When the Time is Right to Have Intercourse?

Elizabeth Winship, through her nationally syndicated column "Ask Beth," has for many years given advice to thousands of young people. In 1983 she wrote an excellent book, *Reaching Your Teenager.* I recommend that you read it. In the book she lists the important questions to which you ought to be able to answer yes before you have intercourse.* As Beth says, "This is a tough test to pass. However, people who can pass it will seldom have any ill effects from sexual relations."

Are You Ready?

• *Are you really grown up physically? Teenagers go through puberty by age fourteen or fifteen and can perform the act of intercourse far earlier than that. True physical maturation, however, isn't usually reached until seventeen, eighteen, or even later.*

• *Are you really mature emotionally? It takes patience, self-control, and understanding for two people to have mutually enjoyable sexual relations.*

continued

• Are you really knowledgeable about sexuality, and how it works for both males and females? The psychological and sexual consequences of first intercourse are far more important and longer lasting than other "first impressions."

• Do you have enough confidence in yourself to be able to share your most inner self with someone else? It is not easy to surrender one's individuality for the mutual intimacy of intercourse.

• Do you know about reliable birth control measures and are you definitely going to use them?

• Do you accept the responsibility for possible consequences, either accidental pregnancy or venereal disease? This means having both the information and the courage to get help in case either should occur.

• Do you and your partner have a committed, mutually kind and understanding relationship, so that you will give each other consideration and pleasure, not pain?

• Are your motives for intercourse pleasure, fun, and closeness? Wanting sex to please your partner, keep up your status with peers, prove you are grown up, or "get over" virginity are not good enough reasons.

• Are you really looking for intimacy and affection? You may find it in addition to sex, but sex can also be an empty, physical exercise.

• Do you have a safe and comfortable environment, so you won't be hasty and furtive in your lovemaking?

• Do you honestly approve of this for yourself morally? Lingering guilt is still the one thing most likely to sour an early sexual experience. Again, it takes considerable maturity to search your mind and know truthfully what you believe.

*Printed with permission from Beth Winship and Houghton Mifflin Company.

One key to a good sexual relationship is good communication. If your partner is not willing to respect your reasons for not having intercourse and is not willing to listen to you, that's a sure sign that now is not the time.

Sex: The Media

One hard reality of the world of teenagers (and adults) today is the sexual influence of popular songs, advertising, movies, and TV. Many of the songs, especially when stereoed in both ears for hours on end, tend to shut out the real world and promote the feeling that sexual activity and intercourse are pretty much everything. You need to be aware of this effect so you don't get snowed.

Advertising, wherever it appears, often uses sex, and especially the female body, to sell products. In effect the ads say, "Wear this [or spray this on, or ride in this, or give this] and you'll have it made sexually." You need to be aware of these distorted messages, especially the false message that to "have it made" sexually is all there is in life, or the false message that a mere product can "make it" for you.

Probably the most powerful influence on people is TV because it's always there in the intimacy of the home. It often starts exerting its influence, five to ten hours a day, on children at a very young age. TV is the baby-sitter for many young kids. It's hard to fight TV because it absorbs you and just keeps on going. You can't stop it and argue with it. And the sexual messages from TV advertising aren't based on reality, they are designed to sell products. In addition, without directly saying so, the stories on widely watched TV programs promote the idea that most sexual activity takes place outside of marriage. A recent count of soap operas showed that 94 percent of all copulations took place between people not married to each other, and a very large amount of sex was suggested—about two intimate sexual acts per hour in the average program. The head of one network was worried that his corporation would make less money because its sex-act-per-hour rate was lower than the rate of two other networks!

It's difficult for young people (and older people, too) to separate TV fantasy from reality. The fantasy is: "It's O.K. to hop into bed with anyone you want to, and nothing much happens but fun." The hard reality, as you will know if you think clearly, is that it's *not* O.K. and that a lot *more* happens than just fun.

Let's state again some important considerations:

People should not feel pushed into sexual activity or intercourse by their friends or the customs of their group. There are many teenagers who do not want to engage in physical expressions of affection or who are quite embarrassed by them. They would prefer to wait until they have grown up more; they may have other, keener interests; they may not yet feel ready for the emotional effects. You should value yourself too highly to be pressured into sexual activity you do not want. Are you really afraid that people will think you are square or not "with it" unless you are sexually active?

Sexual intercourse is for most people a deeply moving experience, not something to be casually played around with. It can't help but involve not only the body but also the mind and the emotions—one's deepest self. It is also nature's means for carrying on the human race. These facts explain why, when a couple have intercourse as an expression of their love for and commitment to each other, it can bring them even closer together.

But when two people do not care about each other, they may feel guilty or ashamed after having intercourse. This is especially true of girls. When sexual intercourse is undertaken too lightly, it goes against the customs and moral feelings developed through many generations of our culture. If such feelings are deeply ingrained in people as a part of their upbringing, **premarital intercourse** (intercourse before marriage) may result in their not feeling quite right about themselves, and it may make it more difficult for them, later on, to take part in a good, happy sexual relationship within marriage.

However, there are no reliable statistics that show that people who have premarital intercourse are more or less likely to have successful and happy marriages than those who do not. True, there are many people who make confident statements on this matter—either for or against premarital intercourse—but their statements are more matters of personal belief or of what they think ought to be the case than they are statements of fact.

The major religions in the United States teach that it is morally wrong to have sexual intercourse outside of marriage. Fortunately, many churches today provide sex and family-life education programs to help young people deal responsibly with their sexuality. When people's religions do teach that premarital intercourse is wrong and people disregard the teaching, they may very well feel guilty, and this feeling may isolate them from a source of strength, comfort, and confidence that would help them.

A young unmarried couple who produce a child they do not want and are not prepared to care for may feel forced into marriage by family or church. If they marry it will probably not be because after deep consideration they have chosen each other as life partners. Before long the boy and girl may feel angry at each other for all of the difficulty that has been caused. The divorce rate among such young couples is unusually high, and divorce usually leaves a baby and its mother to struggle alone; and a young father is left with the legal obligation, unless his former wife marries again, to support them in addition to the second wife and family he may eventually have.

One other possible consequence of sexual intercourse, especially casual intercourse with several partners, is sexually transmitted disease, VD.

I have placed more emphasis on the problems and possibly unhappy consequences of sexual activity entered into thoughtlessly and irresponsibly than on the pleasures and deep satisfactions growing from sexual relationships based on mature thinking, consideration, caring, and genuine love. This is because I am convinced that to manage the responsibilities of your life you need to know both the bad news and the good news about sex and social life. And this leads us to the last chapter.

CHAPTER SEVENTEEN

Love and sex and life

If you are like most people, your whole life, including your sex life and your experiences with love, will have its ups and downs, its great joys and its sorrows and regrets. Much depends on how you take what life brings you and the values by which you make your decisions. I am talking about both life in adolescence and life later as an adult, whether or not you marry.

And by the way, I hope you will not let yourself be hurried into marriage too soon. There are many people who benefit by waiting to get married, and there are many who probably should never marry at all, or who have never found a person as pleasing to them as the rewards of living singly or in a group. A successful, attractive, loving, lovable, older Quaker lady, a member of my Friends meeting, smilingly said to a friend when she was asked why she had never married: "Well, thee knows, it takes a mighty good husband to be better than none."

Probably most of us know unmarried people who live full, satisfying lives because they have found that the deep and rewarding demands of a career are more important than the satisfactions of marriage, which for some people might prevent the fullest accomplishment in a career.

Questions about career, marriage, and having or not having children, about the conduct of your sexual life, are questions you will be deciding for yourself. All through your life, but especially during your adolescence, you will be searching for your own set of values to guide you. One of the signs of maturity is having developed a sound set of values, even though the search for values should never stop. In Chapter 2, I suggested some values to guide you. This was before you had read all of the information, facts, questions, and opinions contained in this book. Now you may want to consider those values again, to talk about them, and to move ahead toward establishing your own. The values I suggested were: (1) the infinite worth of each individual person, (2) consideration, (3) communication, (4) the family, (5) responsibility, (6) pleasure and good feelings, (7) control, and (8) information. How do these values strike you now? Would you change your order of importance? Can you add any to the list? Would you remove any?

And now, a last word about love and sex. Remember that love is a complicated relationship, and that sexual love is only one part of it. There are other loves: the unreserved support and loyalty found between many parents and their children; the easy comfortableness and enjoyment that come from the love of a friend; the zest and stimulation that are a kind of love felt by people who share common tasks, interests, and problems. I know a young married couple who are happy and satisfied together. The wife expressed the most important aspect of their marriage thus: "We are very-best-friends; we enjoy each other's company more entirely than anyone else's; we have each other to come home to and tell our adventures in the big world. We are sure that without this aspect we would have much less, and that there is nothing else more important in our relationship."

When two people have great affection for each other and understand each other well, and when they make a commitment to join their lives and to care for each other through thick and thin, "for better or for worse," then the sexual part of their love, each for the other, can grow ever more satisfying, joyful, and deep.

Glossary

Words appearing in **boldface** throughout the text are defined in this glossary. If you need to know what a special word means, you can find it here. The number after each entry is, in most cases, the page of the text on which the word or phrase first appears.

abdomen *(AB-doe-men)*.   That part of the human body often called the belly. It contains the stomach, intestines, bladder, and in the female, the uterus, in which the baby grows, and other organs. Page 6.

abortion *(uh-BOR-shun)*.   The removal from the uterus of an embryo or fetus. Page 85.

abstinence *(AB-stin-nens)*.   To abstain from—not to have— sexual intercourse. Page 74.

adolescence *(ad-uh-LESS-ens)*.   The period between puberty and adulthood during which people grow into adults. Page 12.

afterbirth.   The placenta and two amniotic coverings that are pushed out of the uterus right after the birth of the baby. Page 44.

AIDS.   Acquired *i*mmune *d*eficiency *s*yndrome, a rare but deadly sexually transmitted disease that causes people to lose their resistance to disease. Page 94.

amniotic fluid *(am-nee-AH-tik)*.   A clear liquid in a special amniotic sac in the uterus. This liquid surrounds and protects the developing baby during pregnancy. Page 43.

anus *(AY-nus)*.   The opening leading from the intestines to outside the body. Bowel movements pass through the anus. (*Anal* refers to the anus.) Page 8.

basal body temperature (BBT). The temperature of the body upon waking, which, taken regularly, helps a woman know that she has ovulated. Page 79.

Billings Ovulation Method. A method of natural family planning that teaches how to monitor the changes in a woman's cervical mucus secretion which indicate fertility and infertility. Page 78.

birth canal. The passage through which a baby is born (the cervix and vagina). Page 7.

birth control. Control of the number of children born, especially by preventing or reducing the frequency of conception (fertilization). Page 70.

birth control pills *("the pill")*. Pills taken by mouth that prevent a woman from ovulating and becoming pregnant. Page 74.

bisexual *(bye-SEK-shu-whl).* A person who is attracted to people of both sexes. Page 58.

bladder. The sac in which urine is stored to be urinated through the urethra. Page 16.

calendar method. A method of birth control that involves keeping a record of the date on which a woman's menstrual period occurs, which may help her estimate when she will ovulate or has ovulated. Page 79.

cell division. The means by which the fertilized egg grows from a single cell at conception to a baby at birth. Page 33.

cervical mucus *(SER-vi-kel MYU-kus).* Mucus (slippery, moist, clear substance) secreted from the cervix at the vulva area for a few days before and at the time of ovulation. It helps keep sperm alive inside a woman's body. Evaluation of cervical mucus is one of the methods used in natural family planning. Page 78.

cervical os *(ohs).* The opening from the cervix to the vagina. It changes position and texture when ovulation is about to take place. Noticing its condition is one of the methods used in natural family planning. Page 79.

cervix *(SER-vix).* The lower portion of the uterus which extends downward into the vagina. Page 25.

chancre *(SHANK-er).* A small sore, symptom of syphilis. Page 93.

chlamydia *(kla-MID-ia).* The organism that causes most cases of nongonoccal urethritis (NGU). Page 92.

chromosomes *(KRO-mo-sohms)*. Very small rod-shaped bodies that transmit the heredity of people from one generation to the next by means of genes. Page 28.

circumcision *(ser-kum-SIH-shun)*. A surgical operation that removes the foreskin of the penis. After circumcision a male is said to be circumcised. Page 16.

clitoris *(KLIH-ter-us)*. A small, very sexually sensitive female organ located just above a woman's urethra and covered by a hood called the labia (lips). Page 11.

coitus *(KOH-eh-tus)*. See **sexual intercourse.**

colostrum *(kuh-LAHS-trum)*. The yellowish, watery fluid that a baby sucks from its mother's breast for a day or two after birth. Page 46.

conceive. To become pregnant. Page 30.

conception. The moment of fertilization, when sperm joins egg. Page 30. See **fertilization.**

condom *(KAHN-dum)*. A thin finger-shaped rubber device placed over the erect penis to prevent the escape of sperm into the vagina and thus to prevent pregnancy. Page 77.

contraception *(kahn-truh-SEP-shun)*. Using a method or device to prevent pregnancy, that is, to prevent a sperm from fertilizing an egg, which is called conception. Page 70.

contraceptive sponge. A plastic sponge containing sperm-killing chemicals. A woman places it in her uterus before having sexual intercourse to prevent fertilization. Page 77.

contractions *(kuhn-TRAK-shuns)*. The action of the muscles of the uterus that help to push the baby out through the cervix and vagina in childbirth. Page 42.

copulation *(cahp-you-LAY-shun)*. Mating or sexual coupling between animals. With human beings it is called sexual intercourse. Page 48.

crabs (crab lice). A kind of insect that gets into the pubic hair and causes itching. The lice are passed from one person to another during close genital contact. Page 95.

diaphragm *(DYE-uh-fram)*. A rubber cap placed in the vagina, over the entrance to the cervix, to prevent sperm from entering and thus to prevent pregnancy. Page 76.

differentiation *(dif-er-en-shee-AY-shun)*. The complicated organizing and development of cells so as to create the different parts of the body during the development of the baby in the uterus. Page 33.

DNA. A chemical, deoxyribonucleic acid, that contains the genes that determine the inherited characteristics of forms of life, including human beings. Page 28.

ejaculation *(ee-jak-you-LAY-shun)*. The spurting out of semen from the penis. Page 19.

embryo *(EM-bree-oh)*. The growing fertilized egg from conception until the end of the third month of pregnancy. After that it is called a fetus. Page 33.

endometrium *(en-doh-MEE-tree-um)*. The soft velvety lining of the uterus. Page 7.

environment *(en-VYE-ruhn-ment)*. The conditions (people, things, circumstances) by which one is surrounded. (Often contrasted with heredity.) Page 29.

epididymis *(ep-ih-DID-ih-miss)*. A collection of tiny tubes behind each testicle in which sperm cells are matured as they pass through, and are stored. Page 18.

erection *(ih-REK-shun)*. The hardening and enlarging of the penis that occurs when a man is sexually stimulated, and at other times. Page 19.

estrogen *(ES-tro-jen)*. A hormone produced by the ovaries that produces female sex characteristics and affects the menstrual cycle. Page 57.

fallopian tubes *(fah-LOW-pee-an)*. The tubes that lead from near each ovary to the uterus, and down which the egg travels. Page 6.

family planning. Planning how many children a family wants and can provide for, how far apart they should be spaced, and using birth control to carry out the plans. Page 70.

fertility *(fer-TIL-ih-tee)*. The state of being fertile—that is, capable of becoming pregnant (in a woman) or of impregnating (in a man). Page 78.

fertility awareness. Factual and personal knowledge of the symptoms of fertility as they occur in a woman's body. Specifically, this means being able to recognize the approach and passage of ovulation. Page 78.

fertilization *(fer-til-eye-ZA-shun)*. The moment when a sperm joins an egg (ovum) and an embryo is formed. It is also called the moment of conception, when a new life is conceived. Page 30.

fetal alcohol syndrome *(FEE-tuhl)*. A serious disorder appearing in babies born to mothers who drink heavily while they are pregnant. It causes deformities and mental retardation. Page 38.

fetus *(FEE-tuss)*. The growing unborn baby from the third month after conception until birth. Page 33.

fimbria *(FIM-bree-ah)*. The fingerlike fringes at the end of each fallopian tube that help the egg go into the tube for its journey to the uterus. Page 6.

foreplay. The beginning stages of sexual intercourse during which the couple sexually stimulate each other before the penis enters the vagina. Page 25.

foreskin. The skin covering the top of the penis. In some males it is removed by circumcision, usually when they are infants. Page 16.

fraternal twins. Twins that are each started by the union of a separate sperm and egg. The twins do not look any more alike than do other brothers and sisters. Page 40.

gender. Male or female. Page 31.

gender identity. The awareness a person has of being either male or female, feeling yourself male or feeling yourself female. Page 55.

genes *(jeens)*. The basic units of heredity, carried by the chromosomes. Page 28.

genetics *(jeh-NEH-tix)*. The science of heredity, of how traits are passed by genes from one generation to the next. Page 29.

genital herpes. See **herpes.**

genitals *(JEN-ih-tels)*. The sexual organs, especially the external sexual parts. Pages 6, 16.

gestation *(jess-TAY-shun)*. The period between conception and birth of a baby—about 266 days, just under nine months, in human beings. Page 32.

gonococcus *(gonn-uh-KAH-kuss)*. The bacterium that causes gonorrhea. Page 89.

gonorrhea *(gonn-uh-REE-uh)*. A common but serious venereal disease. Page 89.

growth spurt. The period of extra-rapid growth during a boy's or girl's adolescence. Page 9.

gynecologist *(gye-nuh-KAHL-oh-jist)*. A doctor who specializes in the health problems of women, especially those having to do with the reproductive system. Page 12.

heat. In female animals, the period when copulation, or mating, will result in pregnancy. Page 48.

heredity. Characteristics that are passed from parents to child through the union of sperm and egg by the genes in each. Page 28.

herpes (genital herpes) *(JEN-ih-tel HER-pees).* A very common sexually transmitted disease. Page 89.

heterosexual *(HEH-ter-oh-SEK-shu-uhl).* Having to do with the other sex; attracted to people of the other sex. Page 58.

homophobia *(hoe-moe-PHOE-bee-uh).* A strong, unreasoning fear of homosexuality and homosexual people. Page 60.

homosexual. Having to do with the same sex; attracted to people of the same sex. Page 58.

hormones. Chemicals which glands secrete into the bloodstream and which play a part in causing sex differences between men and women. Page 56.

hymen *(HYE-men).* The very thin layer of tissue that partially closes the entrance to the vagina in most females who have not had sexual intercourse or used tampons. Page 13.

identical twins. Twins that are started when a single fertilized egg divides into two parts and each part then develops independently alike. Page 40.

illegitimate child *(il-lee-JIT-ih-muht).* A child born of unmarried parents. Page 71.

incest. Intimate sexual relations between people who are close relatives. Page 66.

instinct. A natural, inherited impulse or capacity. Page 49.

intercourse. See **sexual intercourse.**

intrauterine device *(in-truh-YOU-ter-in).* See **IUD.**

IUD. Intrauterine device. A coil, loop, or T-shaped device placed in the uterus to prevent conception and/or implantation of a fertilized egg. Page 75.

labia *(LAY-bee-uh).* The lips of the female genitals. The labia enfold the clitoris and are a part of the vulva. Page 11.

labor. The process of delivery of the fetus from the uterus at the end of pregnancy. Page 42.

laparoscopy *(LAP-uh-RAH-sko-pee).* The means of sterilization using a miniature telescope and cauterizer inserted through an incision in the navel. Thus the doctor may see the fallopian tubes and perform a tubal ligation. Page 81.

lesbian *(LEZ-bee-uhn)*. A female homosexual person. Page 58.

making out. Physical contact beyond hand-holding and light kissing. May include petting and sexual intercourse. Page 105.

masturbation. Stimulation of the sex organs for pleasure. Page 22.

menopause. The time in a woman's life when she stops ovulating and menstruating. (Sometimes called "change of life.") Page 14.

menstrual cycle *(MEN-stroo-uhl)*. The more-or-less regular female fertility cycle beginning with the first day of menstruation and continuing for about a month until the next menstruation. Page 6.

menstrual period. Three- to six-day period when menstruation occurs. Page 14.

menstruation *(MEN-stroo-AY-shun)*. The monthly discharge of blood and lining from the uterus, does not occur if the ovum is fertilized. Page 9.

midwife. A person trained to help women during childbirth. Page 42.

molester *(mo-LESS-tur)*. A person who molests or abuses children in order to satisfy his or her sexual desires. Page 66.

"morning-after" pill. A very strong estrogen pill which can prevent pregnancy if taken within 24 hours to 72 hours after intercourse. Causes vomiting, diarrhea, and headaches. Page 82.

mucus *(MYU-kus)*. A wet, slippery substance produced by various parts of the body, including the cervix. Page 12.

Natural Family Planning (NFP). Methods of birth control based upon knowledge of the time when a woman has ovulated. These include the cervical mucus method, basal body temperature method (BBT), cervical self-exam, and calendar method. Page 78.

navel. The small scar where the umbilical cord is attached, often called the belly button. Page 8.

necking. Light expressions of physical affection such as sitting close, holding hands, light kissing. Page 105.

nipple. The tip of the breast. Babies suck milk from their mother's nipples, called nursing. Page 46.

nocturnal emission *(nahk-TER-nul ee-MIH-shun)*. Ejaculat-

ing semen while asleep or nearly asleep. Often called a "wet dream."
Page 21.

nongonococcal urethritis (NGU) *(nahn-gahn-uh-KAH-kull yer-eh-THRYE-tuss)*. A very common sexually transmitted disease (not gonorrhea). Page 89.

obstetrician *(ahb-steh-TRIH-shun)*. A doctor who specializes in the care of pregnant women and in helping them give birth to children. Page 42.

orgasm. The climax of sexual pleasure ("coming"). Page 25.

os. See **cervical os.**

ovaries *(OH-vuh-reez)*. The two female sex organs in which the ova (eggs) are stored, and from which one egg is ovulated (released) about once a month. Page 6.

ovulation *(ah-vyu-LAY-shun)*. The release, about once a month, of an ovum (egg) from an ovary. Page 6.

ovum (plural, **ova**). The egg cell. Page 6.

parenting. The activities involved with being the parent of a child or children; bringing up, caring for, and nurturing children. Page 72.

pelvic inflammatory disease (PID). A serious disease of the uterus and fallopian tubes. Page 92.

penis. The principal male sex organ. Page 16.

petting. Deep kissing and caressing the most sensitive parts of the body. Page 105.

pill, the. See **birth control pills.**

pituitary gland *(pih-TOO-ih-ter-ree)*. The master gland or "time clock" that largely controls the functioning of other glands and determines the timing and order of events during adolescent development. It is located at the base of the brain. Page 9.

placenta *(pluh-SEN-tuh)*. A structure that forms in the uterus, by means of which the developing baby receives its nourishment and gets rid of its waste. It is connected to the fetus by the umbilical cord. Page 33.

pregnant. Carrying a fertilized egg within the uterus, where it will develop into a baby. Page 12.

premarital intercourse. Sexual intercourse before marriage. Page 112.

premature baby. A baby born before the normal end of pregnancy. Page 36.

prenatal care *(PREE-nay-tuhl)*. Caring for a pregnant woman and the embryo or fetus growing in her womb. Page 72.

progesterone *(pro-JESS-ter-ohn)*. The female "pregnancy hormone" that prepares the uterus to receive the fertilized egg and the breasts to produce milk. Page 57.

prostate gland. A gland that surrounds the male urethra. It secretes milky fluid, a part of the semen, and the muscles around it are the main source of power of ejaculation. Page 18.

puberty *(PYU-ber-tee)*. The period during which a boy or girl enters adolescence. For girls, it is marked by the first menstruation; for boys, by the first ejaculation of semen. After puberty, a girl can become pregnant and a boy can impregnate a girl. Page 6.

pubic hair. The curly hair that grows just above the penis in a boy, and on the upper part of and also above the vulva in a girl. Pages 11, 21.

quickening. The first faint sign of activity of the baby in its mother's womb, usually at about four months. Page 34.

rape. Sexual intercourse forced by one person upon another, usually by a man upon a woman; an act of violence using sex as a weapon. Page 67.

reproduction *(ree-pro-DUK-shun)*. Producing babies, beginning with sexual intercourse or copulation. Page 48.

rhythm method *(RIH-them)*. See **calendar method**.

rutty. Being sexually aroused by a female in heat. Used in referring to male animals. Page 48.

scrotum *(SKRO-tum)*. The sac of loose crinkly skin that hangs under a man's penis and contains the testicles. Page 18.

secondary sex characteristics. The body characteristics (other than reproductive organs) that develop during puberty, such as pubic hair, beard, underarm hair, breasts, deepening of the voice, and changing body shape. Page 57.

semen *(SEE-men)*. Fluid containing sperm. It is ejaculated from the penis during a man's orgasm. Page 19.

seminal vesicles *(SEM-ih-nal VEH-sih-kels)*. Two small pouches at the back of the prostate gland in which semen is stored. Page 18.

sex role. Society's ideas of how a male or a female ought to behave. Page 55.

sexual intercourse *(SEK-shu-uhl IN-ter-korss)* (also called

coitus). The mating of a man and a woman, when his erect penis enters her vagina, usually resulting in the ejaculation of semen. Sexual intercourse is the way babies are started and is also a major source of sexual pleasure. Page 24.

sexuality *(sek-shu-AL-ih-tee)*. Our sexual nature; the part of our lives that has to do with our being male or female. Page 52.

sexually transmitted disease (STD). Any of a number of diseases transmitted by sexual intercourse or other intimate body contact such as deep kissing or heavy petting. Often called venereal disease (VD). Page 88.

sperm. The male reproductive cell, made in the testicles, shaped like a tadpole. When it fertilizes an ovum, a baby is started. Page 16.

spermicide. A substance that when placed in the vagina before intercourse kills the sperm. Page 76.

spermatozoa *(sper-MAT-uh-zoh-uh)*. Scientific name for sperm cells. Page 20.

sponge. See **contraceptive sponge.**

spirochetes *(SPY-ro-keets)*. Small corkscrew-shaped organisms that cause syphilis. Page 92.

sterility. The state of being unable to impregnate or become pregnant; that is, unable to produce a child. Page 90.

sterilization *(ster-ill-eye-ZAY-shun)*. A surgical operation to prevent a man from impregnating or a woman from becoming pregnant. Page 80. (See **vasectomy; tubal ligation.**)

syphilis *(SIH-fill-iss)*. A very serious venereal disease, now easily curable. Page 89.

tampon. A small roll of absorbent material inserted into the vagina to absorb the menstrual flow. Page 13.

testicle *(TES-tih-kel)* (plural: testicles or **testes**). One of two oval-shaped glands that manufacture sperm. The testes are contained in the scrotum. Page 18.

testosterone *(tes-TOSS-ter-ohn)*. A hormone which is secreted by the testicles in men and by the adrenal glands in men and women. It is made in larger quantities in male bodies than in female bodies and tends to cause vigorous behavior; it also makes secondary sex characteristics, such as the beard and a muscularly strong body. Page 57.

toxic shock syndrome. A rare disease among women mainly

caused by failure to change menstrual pads or tampons frequently enough. Page 13.

trichomonas (**trichomoniasis**) *(trik-oh-MOW-nus, trik-oh-muh-NYE-uh-suss)*. A very common sexually transmitted disease. Page 89.

trimester *(try-MESS-ter)*. A three-month period of time. The nine months of a woman's pregnancy are commonly divided into the first, second, and third trimesters. Page 33.

tubal ligation *(TOO-bel lye-GAY-shun)*. A surgical operation that cuts and ties off the fallopian tubes so that no egg can pass from ovary to uterus; a method of sterilization. Page 81.

tubal pregnancy (also called **ectopic pregnancy**). A very serious condition when a fertilized egg is blocked on the way down the fallopian tube and thus begins to grow in the tube rather than the uterus. Page 90.

umbilical cord *(um-BILL-ih-kel)*. The ropelike cord connecting the growing baby to the placenta inside the mother's womb. Page 33.

urethra *(yu-REE-thruh)*. The tube through which urine passes out of the bladder during urination. Also, a male ejaculates semen through his urethra. Page 16.

urinary infection. One of several kinds of infection that causes painful urination. Page 94.

uterus *(YU-ter-us)* (also called **womb**). The organ in which a fertilized ovum (egg) grows into a baby, ready to be born. It is also the organ from which the menstrual fluid is discarded. Page 7.

vagina *(va-JYE-nuh)*. The soft, muscular passageway between the uterus and the outside of a woman's body. Page 7.

vas deferens *(vas DEF-er-ens)*. One of two tubes through which the sperm pass from the testicles toward the seminal vesicles, ready to be ejaculated (often called simply the vas). Page 18.

vasectomy *(va-SEK-tuh-mee)*. A surgical operation that cuts a short section from each vas deferens and ties off the ends so that no sperm are carried to the semen; a method of sterilization. Page 80.

venereal disease (**VD**) *(vuh-NEER-ee-uhl)*. See **sexually transmitted disease (STD)**.

viable *(VYE-uh-bel)*. Able to live and develop normally, as a newborn infant. Page 86.

virgin.   A person who has not had sexual intercourse. More often used to refer to females. Page 14.

vulva.   The area of the external female sex organs, including the lips (labia) enfolding the clitoris. After puberty it is covered with pubic hair. Page 11.

wet dream.   See **nocturnal emission.**

withdrawal.   A method of birth control in which a man withdraws his penis from the woman's vagina before he ejaculates semen. Page 80.

womb *(woom).*   See **uterus.**

yeast infections.   One of several sexual diseases causing itching and a burning sensation in the vagina. Page 94.

Mastery Test*

You may have read this book at home, or perhaps you used it at school as a part of a course or unit of study. In any case, it will be useful for you to know whether or not you have learned the basic facts and ideas. That's why this test is provided.

It doesn't matter if you look at the test and study for it in advance of taking it. After all, in doing so you'll be studying and learning important factual information, and that's the point. If the test is used in school and the results are counted as part of your grade, then the pages should be duplicated and given to you separately from the book, as any other school test would be.

1. **The ovaries**
    A. are two of a woman's reproductive organs.
    B. are where the baby grows for nine months.
    C. contain thousands of undeveloped egg cells.
    D. are the organs from which mature eggs are ovulated.

2. **The menstrual cycle**
    A. lasts the same number of days in all women.
    B. includes menstruation.
    C. includes ovulation.
    D. stops during the time a woman is pregnant.

3. **The fallopian tubes**
    A. are a passage between the ovaries and the uterus.
    B. provide a passage along which the egg travels after ovulation.
    C. are the place where the actual fertilization of the egg takes place.
    D. are a part of the birth canal.

*The publishers hereby grant permission to reproduce pages 129–138 to be used for testing purposes in schools or elsewhere. Permission is also given to duplicate the answer sheet on page 139.

4. **Ovulation**
   A. occurs when a woman becomes pregnant.
   B. is the release of an egg from an ovary about once a month.
   C. stops when a woman reaches menopause.
   D. is necessary if a woman is to conceive.

5. **The uterus**
   A. is the organ in which the egg is fertilized by the sperm.
   B. is the place where the fertilized egg grows into a baby.
   C. develops a soft lining in which a fertilized egg is implanted.
   D. has powerful muscles which help push the baby out during birth.

6. **An ovum is**
   A. an egg cell.
   B. what is released from an ovary during ovulation.
   C. a very small baby with all its parts in miniature.
   D. what is fertilized by a sperm.

7. **Menstruation**
   A. occurs when the uterus sheds its lining.
   B. is a sign that a woman is not pregnant.
   C. usually lasts from 3 to 6 days.
   D. is just like simple bleeding from a cut.

8. **The following are parts of the puberty "timetable" for girls:**
   A. a growth spurt
   B. an enlargement of the breasts
   C. a sudden increase in scores on intelligence tests
   D. the growth of pubic hair

9. **A woman's genital area includes**
   A. the breasts.
   B. the lips of the vagina.
   C. the pubic hair.
   D. the clitoris.

10. **A woman is pregnant if she**
    A. is carrying a fertilized egg in her uterus.
    B. can expect to give birth to a baby, assuming normal development.
    C. will soon get married and wants to have children.
    D. has conceived.

11. **When a woman menstruates,**
    A. she usually uses a pad or tampon to absorb the fluid.
    B. she may sometimes feel some pain in the abdomen or the lower back.
    C. she should change pads or tampons frequently, according to instructions.
    D. she must go to a clinic or hospital for special care.

12. **When a woman reaches menopause,**
    A. her ovaries no longer discharge eggs.
    B. she can no longer enjoy sexual intercourse.
    C. she cannot become pregnant.
    D. she no longer menstruates.

13. **The penis**
    A. is a man's most obvious sexual organ.
    B. sometimes becomes erect.
    C. is located just below the testicles.
    D. contains a passageway for urine and semen.

14. **An erection of the penis**
    A. means that a man must have sexual intercourse at once.
    B. is caused by a quick flow of blood into the tissues of the penis.
    C. may be stimulated by many different things, not just bodily contact with another person.
    D. makes it possible for a man to have sexual intercourse.

15. **During an ejaculation,**
    A. from 100 to 500 million sperm are discharged from the penis.
    B. about a spoonful of semen comes out of the penis.
    C. a man experiences a strong feeling of pleasure.
    D. urine combines with semen, and this may be harmful.

16. **The following are changes that occur as a boy passes through puberty:**
    A. an increase in sharpness of eyesight
    B. a change of voice
    C. a spurt of growth
    D. the growth of pubic hair

17. During sexual intercourse,
     A. a man's penis enters a woman's vagina.
     B. semen is ejaculated, which may cause pregnancy.
     C. a woman and a man may feel a special closeness to each other.
     D. it is rare for a man or woman to experience much pleasure.

18. The following are ways of saying that a woman has a baby developing inside her:
     A. She has conceived.
     B. She has had sexual intercourse.
     C. She is pregnant.
     D. She is in her gestation period.

19. Whether a baby will be a boy or a girl
     A. is determined by the sperm, not the ovum.
     B. is decided permanently once fertilization has occurred.
     C. is determined by whether one chromosome is Y or X.
     D. is determined by how well fed the mother is during pregnancy.

20. The period between the conception and the birth of a baby
     A. is called the period of gestation.
     B. is exactly the same length in all woman for each birth.
     C. can be divided into three trimesters.
     D. usually lasts about nine months.

21. While the baby is developing inside the uterus, it
     A. is attached to the placenta by means of the umbilical cord.
     B. is not affected by what its mother eats or drinks.
     C. receives nourishment through the umbilical cord.
     D. makes its own blood, which does not mix with its mother's blood.

22. The following are true statements about a baby developing inside the uterus:
     A. For the first three months, it is called an embryo.
     B. For about the last six months, it is called a fetus.
     C. It tastes the food its mother eats at each meal.
     D. For a time, it is covered with downy hair.

23. The following are true statements about the development of a baby in the uterus:
  A. If its mother smokes, it is likely to be born less healthy than if its mother does not smoke.
  B. If its mother eats no meat, it is unlikely to be able to eat and digest meat during its whole life.
  C. If its mother is a heavy drinker of alcohol, the baby is more likely to be born retarded or deformed than if its mother is not a drinker.
  D. If its mother is addicted to heroin, the baby will be born addicted.

24. The following statements about twins are facts:
  A. One birth in every ninety or so produces twins.
  B. Fraternal twins are the product of two eggs, each fertilized by a different sperm.
  C. Identical twins are the product of one fertilized egg which divides into two embryos after fertilization.
  D. Identical twins are sometimes both boys or both girls, or sometimes a boy and a girl.

25. The process of giving birth to a baby
  A. involves labor, which can be painful.
  B. will probably involve less anxiety on the part of the mother if she understands just what will happen.
  C. is usually attended by an obstetrician or a midwife.
  D. is usually painless and quite easy if the mother is well trained.

26. Soon after a baby is born,
  A. the uterus pushes out the placenta and other parts of the afterbirth.
  B. its umbilical cord is painlessly cut.
  C. it reaches out its hands and tries to get back inside its mother again.
  D. it takes its first breath of air, usually letting out a small, high cry.

27. The following are true of babies just after they are born:
  A. They are usually rather wrinkled and splotchy, and not very beautiful.

B. They should not be held or cuddled because they can be damaged by so doing.

C. They can tell light from dark but cannot see clearly.

D. They are very good at sucking and will suck on almost anything.

28. The following are differences between human sex and animal sex:

A. For human beings, sex is attractive and urgent, but for most animals it is not.

B. Most animals copulate only when the female is in heat.

C. Human beings decide when they are going to engage in sexual activity; most animals know only by instinct.

D. Human beings are "responsible" for their sexual actions; animals are not.

29. The following are true statements about human sexuality:

A. It means more than just sex.

B. It means all that goes with the fact of being a boy or girl, or man or woman.

C. It means that the more sexual activity one engages in, the better human being one is.

D. It is partly inborn, partly affected by the environment.

30. The following are true statements about homosexuality:

A. The first part of the word comes from the Greek *homos*, meaning "same."

B. Homosexuals agree that being heterosexual or homosexual is a simple matter of choice.

C. Female homosexuals are often called lesbians (from the Greek island of Lesbos).

D. Scientists do not agree on what causes some people to be homosexual, others heterosexual.

31. The following are true statements about sex differences between men and women:

A. In the past fifty years, attitudes toward sex differences in the United States have become more tolerant.

B. All boys are stronger and more aggressive than any girls of the same age.

C. Sex differences are caused in part by the fact that only women can become pregnant and bear children.

D. Sex differences are caused in part by hormones, especially testosterone, estrogen, and progesterone.

32. "Sexuality is more than bodies" means that

A. people express themselves sexually through clothing, manners, interests, and so on.

B. people learn their sexuality in part by the ways they were treated by their parents.

C. human sexuality is a complex combination of many facts and feelings.

D. people should never allow bodily sexual pleasure to be important to them.

33. The following are true statements about masturbation:

A. Masturbation is a major cause of physical disease and mental illness.

B. Masturbation consists of rubbing or stroking the genitals in order to have an orgasm.

C. Many people have sexual thoughts or fantasies while they masturbate.

D. Some religious groups believe that it is a sin or a moral disorder.

34. Some of the ways in which sex can be a problem arise from:

A. people having sex without telling their partner they have a sexually transmitted disease.

B. adults using young children as a means to achieve sexual pleasure.

C. one partner hurrying another into sexual intercourse without considering the other's feelings and needs.

D. partners considering each other as people rather than just as objects to give pleasure.

35. The following are true statements about rape:

A. Rape means sexual intercourse forced by one person on another.

B. In most cases, the person raped is a woman, the rapist a man.

C. A person who has been raped should keep it a secret and never tell anyone.

D. Rapists are dangerous and often mentally ill.

36. **Some special problems of teenage pregnancy are:**
    A. Often, the parents are not mature enough to bring up their children well.
    B. Very young mothers often fail to get good medical care and nutrition.
    C. The father tends to stay around the house and give too much care to the baby.
    D. Having a baby at a very young age may interrupt the parents' plans for education and a career.

37. **The following are very effective methods of birth control:**
    A. abstinence
    B. withdrawal
    C. the pill
    D. condom and foam used together

38. **The following are true statements about natural family planning:**
    A. It is based on "fertility awareness."
    B. It uses no chemicals or artificial means to prevent conception.
    C. It must be used intelligently and carefully.
    D. It is probably the easiest method of birth control to use.

39. **The following are true statements about sterilization:**
    A. Sterilization involves sterilizing the sperm so that they cannot fertilize the egg.
    B. For women, it involves a tubal ligation.
    C. For men, it involves a vasectomy.
    D. Sterilization does not interfere with the enjoyment of sexual intercourse.

40. **The following so-called methods of contraception do *not* work:**
    A. douches
    B. urination right after intercourse
    C. having intercourse only when the woman is menstruating
    D. intrauterine devices (IUDs)

41. If a birth control method is to be used successfully, the users must
    A. learn how to use it correctly.
    B. not tell their partner what method is being used.
    C. remember to use it when the time comes.
    D. be prepared in advance of intercourse to use it.

42. The following are true statements about abortion:
    A. Abortion involves removing the embryo or fetus from the uterus by a surgical procedure.
    B. When done by an expert and early in pregnancy, the operation is quite simple and safe.
    C. The operation usually means that the female will be unable to have any more babies.
    D. Some people believe that abortion is immoral.

43. The following are among the five main sexually transmitted diseases:
    A. acne
    B. herpes
    C. gonorrhea
    D. trichomonas

44. People who think they have a sexually transmitted disease should
    A. be sure to inform any sexual partners.
    B. not tell parents or friends under any circumstances.
    C. go promptly for testing and, if needed, treatment by a doctor or clinic.
    D. follow with great care instructions for treatment.

45. Some common symptoms of sexually transmitted diseases are:
    A. painful sores or blisters on or near the genitals.
    B. intense itching of the genitals.
    C. increased desire for sexual intercourse.
    D. a burning feeling while urinating.

46. Sexual responsibility requires, among other things, the following:
    A. respect for one's own health and feelings
    B. correct information about human sexuality

C. approval of all one's friends before engaging in any kind of sexual activity

D. respect for the health and feelings of others

47. **If a young unmarried couple is involved in petting, they should**
   A. decide in advance how far they are going to go—where they will stop.
   B. remember that it is possible to get so aroused that it is difficult to stop.
   C. each be aware of the feelings of the other.
   D. just relax and enjoy the pleasures no matter what they may lead to.

48. **Some good reasons for some people to say no to sexual intercourse are:**
   A. They just don't feel ready for it at this time in their lives.
   B. They know that sex is dirty and should be engaged in only to produce children.
   C. They realize that having sexual intercourse casually can cause many problems.
   D. They want to save sexual intercourse for marriage.

49. **The following are true statements about premarital intercourse:**
   A. Almost all people who have premarital intercourse have unhappy marriages later on.
   B. The major religions in the United States teach that premarital intercourse is morally wrong.
   C. One of the dangers of premarital intercourse is that it may result in a baby whose parents are not ready to care for it.
   D. The term means having sexual intercourse before marriage.

50. **The following are true statements about love:**
   A. The only kind of important love is sexual love.
   B. An important kind of love is the love of members of a family for each other.
   C. The loyalty, comfort, and enjoyment that friends feel with each other is a kind of love.
   D. The love of a happily married couple who are sharing their lives involves more than sexual love.

Answer Sheet

Name: _____

Date: _____

Directions: Write an X over the letter that represents the one **wrong** answer.

Sample items:

1. Girls are	2. This book is about
A. people.	A. love.
B. trees.	B. sex.
C. female.	C. people.
D. not boys.	D. mountains.

For these sample items, you would mark the answer sheet thus:

1. A ✗ C D
2. A B C ✗

1.	A	B	C	D	18.	A	B	C	D	35.	A	B	C	D
2.	A	B	C	D	19.	A	B	C	D	36.	A	B	C	D
3.	A	B	C	D	20.	A	B	C	D	37.	A	B	C	D
4.	A	B	C	D	21.	A	B	C	D	38.	A	B	C	D
5.	A	B	C	D	22.	A	B	C	D	39.	A	B	C	D
6.	A	B	C	D	23.	A	B	C	D	40.	A	B	C	D
7.	A	B	C	D	24.	A	B	C	D	41.	A	B	C	D
8.	A	B	C	D	25.	A	B	C	D	42.	A	B	C	D
9.	A	B	C	D	26.	A	B	C	D	43.	A	B	C	D
10.	A	B	C	D	27.	A	B	C	D	44.	A	B	C	D
11.	A	B	C	D	28.	A	B	C	D	45.	A	B	C	D
12.	A	B	C	D	29.	A	B	C	D	46.	A	B	C	D
13.	A	B	C	D	30.	A	B	C	D	47.	A	B	C	D
14.	A	B	C	D	31.	A	B	C	D	48.	A	B	C	D
15.	A	B	C	D	32.	A	B	C	D	49.	A	B	C	D
16.	A	B	C	D	33.	A	B	C	D	50.	A	B	C	D
17.	A	B	C	D	34.	A	B	C	D					

Answers:

1. B	11. D	21. B	31. B	41. B
2. A	12. B	22. C	32. D	42. C
3. D	13. C	23. B	33. A	43. A
4. A	14. A	24. D	34. D	44. B
5. A	15. D	25. D	35. C	45. C
6. C	16. A	26. C	36. C	46. C
7. D	17. D	27. B	37. B	47. D
8. C	18. B	28. A	38. D	48. B
9. A	19. D	29. C	39. A	49. A
10. C	20. B	30. B	40. D	50. A

Acknowledgments

The following people read all or parts of the manuscript of the fourth revised edition. I thank them for their invaluable help. Knowledgeable as they all are, they did not always all agree on every point, so the final decisions have been mine. To all of the following goes the credit for many of the strengths of this book and no blame for any of its shortcomings.

Peggy Brick, Englewood, NJ; teacher, Human Behavior, Dwight Morrow High School, Englewood, NJ; consultant, Family Life and Sexuality Education, Affirmative Teaching Associates.

Vern L. Bullough, R.N., Ph.D., Buffalo, NY; Dean, Faculty of Natural and Social Sciences, State University of NY College at Buffalo; past president, Society for the Scientific Study of Sex; author of books and articles on human sexuality.

Mary S. Calderone, M.D., M.P.H., New York City; co-founder and former president of SIECUS (Sex Information and Education Council of the U.S.); Adjunct Professor, Graduate Program in Human Sexuality, New York University; co-author of *The Family Book About Sexuality* and *Talking with Your Child about Sex*.

Willard Cates, Jr., M.D., M.P.H., Atlanta; Director, Division of Venereal Disease Control, Center for Prevention Services, Centers for Disease Control, U.S. Department of Health and Human Services.

Pamela and Joseph Gilchrist, Bensalem, PA; teachers of natural family planning, Family Life Bureau, Philadelphia (for the Natural Family Planning section).

Sarah Blaffer Hardy, Ph.D., Davis, CA; Professor of Anthropology, University of California, Davis; former associate in biological anthropology, Peabody Museum, Harvard University; former associate professor, Rice University, Houston; author of *The Langurs of Abu: Female and Male Strategies of Reproduction* and *The Woman that Never Evolved*.

John L. Kitzmiller, M.D., San Francisco; Chief, Perinatal Service; Associate Professor, Department of Obstetrics, Gynecology, and Reproductive Sciences, University of California, San Francisco.

Nancy Savage LeSage, M.A., Philadelphia; Chairman, Reading Department, Pepper Middle School, Philadelphia Public Schools.

Rob Roy MacGregor, M.D., Philadelphia; Associate Professor of Medicine; Chief, Infectious Diseases Section, University of Pennsylvania School of Medicine.

Kim Marshall, Boston; Manager of Instructional Services, Boston Public Schools; author of *Law and Order in Grade 6-E.*

Robert P. Masland, Jr., M.D., Boston; Chief, Division of Adolescent/Young Adult Medicine, The Children's Hospital, Boston; Associate Professor of Pediatrics, Harvard Medical School, Boston.

Luigi Mastroianni, Jr., M.D., Philadelphia; William Goodell Professor and Department Chairman of Obstetrics and Gynecology, University of Pennsylvania School of Medicine.

Thomas F. Merrifield, Ph.D., Berkeley; psychologist at Counseling Center; Coordinator of Gay Counseling Program, University of California, Berkeley.

Emily H. Mudd, Ph.D., Haverford, PA; Professor Emeritus of Family Study in Psychiatry and Consultant in Behavioral Studies, Department of Obstetrics and Gynecology; University of Pennsylvania School of Medicine; past president of the American Association of Marriage and Family Counselors.

Reba S. Poole, Malvern, PA; Supervisor of Human Growth and Development, School District of Philadelphia; instructor of inservice classes on Human Sexuality and Child Abuse Understanding for educators, parents, and community organizations.

Lawrence S. Weisberg, M.D., Philadelphia; Senior Resident, Department of Medicine, Hospital of the University of Pennsylvania.

Elizabeth Winship, Lincoln, MA; author of nationally syndicated column for teenagers, *Ask Beth*; author of *Ask Beth: You Can't Ask Your Mother, Masculinity and Femininity,* and *Reaching Your Teenager.*

Furthermore, I am grateful to the following people who read earlier editions and whose mark is still on this edition even though they have not read it. The information given about them is as of the date they read the manuscript.

Louise Bates Ames, Ph.D., New Haven; co-founder and co-director, Gesell Institute of Child Development.

Marsha R. Bloom, Philadelphia; Coordinator of Volunteers, Women Organized Against Rape (WOAR).

Warren J. Gadpaille, M.D., Englewood, Colorado; psychoanalyst; Committee on Adolescence of the Group for the Advancement of Psychiatry; consultant in Family Living for Jefferson County School District, CO; Vice-President, American Association of Sex Educators and Counselors, Washington, D.C.; author of *The Cycles of Sex.*

Alan F. Guttmacher, M.D., New York; late Emeritus Clinical Professor of Obstetrics and Gynecology, College of Physicians and Surgeons, Columbia University; President, Planned Parenthood and World Population; author of *Birth Control and Love* (formerly *The Complete Book of Birth Control*), *Understanding Sex: A Young Person's Guide,* and *Pregnancy, Birth and Family Planning.*

W. Meredith Heyl, M.D., Philadelphia; obstetrician and gynecologist to the Germantown and Chestnut Hill hospitals; Assistant Professor of Obstetrics and Gynecology, School of Medicine, Temple University.

Winifred Kempton, Philadelphia; former education director, Planned Parenthood Association of Southeastern Pennsylvania; author of *Techniques for Leading Group Discussions on Human Sexuality.*

Lester A. Kirkendall, Ph.D., Portland, Oregon; Emeritus Professor of Family Life, formerly Oregon State University; author of *Premarital Intercourse and Interpersonal Relations.*

Genevieve Millet Landau, New York City; Editor-in-Chief, *Parents Magazine.*

Harold I. Lief, M.D., Philadelphia; Director, Division of Family Study, Department of Psychiatry, School of Medicine, University of Pennsylvania.

John Money, Ph.D., Baltimore; Professor of Medical Psychology and Associate Professor of Pediatrics, Johns Hopkins University School of Medicine and Hospital; president, 1974–1976, Society for The Scientific Study of Sex; author of *Sex Errors of the Body;* co-author of *Man and Woman, Boy and Girl: The Differentiation and Dimorphism of Gender Identity from Conception to Maturity* and *Sexual Signatures.*

Elaine C. Pierson, M.D., Ph.D., Philadelphia; Office of Gynecology, Student Health Service, University of Pennsylvania; author of *Sex Is Never an Emergency,* and *Female and Male: The Sexual Context.*

Patricia Schiller, M.D., J.D., Washington, D.C.; Executive Director, American Association of Sex Educators, Counselors, and Therapists (AASECT); Assistant Professor, College of Medicine, Howard University.

Walter R. Stokes, LL.B., M.D., Stuart, Florida; retired psychiatrist and sex educator; author of *Married Love in Today's World* and *Modern Pattern for Marriage;* co-author of *45 Levels to Sexual Understanding and Enjoyment.*

Joseph Stokes, Jr., M.D., Philadelphia; late Emeritus Professor of Pediatrics, School of Medicine, University of Pennsylvania; former president, American Pediatric Society.

In addition to those listed, I am grateful to the following people who helped me with the fourth edition in various ways of special value: Patricia Bass, Felix Cayo, Betty Watanabe Endo, Stefanie S. Hufnagel, Gay Gilpin Johnson, Jeffrey G. Johnson, Arnold Relman, Harriet Relman, Daniel Shechtman, Robert Shattuck, Sally Shattuck, Peter Truitt, and Susan Truitt.—E.W.J.

Index

Fallopian tubes, 6
Family, 4–5, 102
Family planning, 70. *See also* Birth
    control (contraception)
    natural (NFP), 78–80
    population and, 73
Fertility awareness, 78
Fertilization, 30–32
Fetal alcoholic syndrome, 38–39
Fetus, 33–39
    syphilis and, 93
Fimbria, 6
Foreplay, 25
Foreskin, 16

Gay people, 58–60
Gender, 31
Gender identity, 55
Genes, 28
Genetics, 29
Genitals
    female, 6
    male, 16–18
Gestation period, 32–33
Gonorrhea, 89–90
Growth spurt
    in boys, 20–21, 23
    in girls, 9–10
Gynecologist, 12

Heredity, 28–29
Herpes (genital herpes), 91
Heterosexuality, 58
Homophobia, 60
Homosexuality, 58–60
Hormones, 56–57
Hymen
    first sexual intercourse and, 27
    tampons and, 13–14

Illegitimate babies, 71
Immoral actions, 101
Inadequacy, feelings of, 64–65
Incest, 66–67
Intercourse, sexual. *See* Sexual
    intercourse
Intrauterine devices (IUDs), 75–76

Jackson, Jesse, 50

Kissing, 105–6

Labia, 11
Labor, 42–43
Language and sex, 68–69
Laparoscopy, 81–82
Lesbians, 58–59
Living together, 115
Love, 24, 26, 102, 112, 116

Making out, 105
Marriage, 102–3, 113, 115
Masturbation, 22, 61–62
Media, the, 111–12
Menopause, 14–15
Menstrual cycle (menstruation), 6, 7, 9,
    11–15
    fertilization and, 31–32
    intercourse during, 83
Midwife, 42
Milk, mother's, 46–47
Molestation of children, 65–66
Moral actions, 101
Morning-after pill, 82
Mucus, cervical, 12

Natural family planning (NFP), 78–80
Navel (belly button), 44
Necking, 105
Newborn babies, 44, 46
Nipples, 46
Nocturnal emission, 21, 23
Nongonococcal urethritis (NGU), 92
Nursing a baby, 46–47

Obstetrician, 42
Oral contraceptives, 74–75
Orgasm, 25–27
Ovaries, 6
Ovulation, 6, 12, 26
Ovum (egg cell), 6–7, 28
    fertilization and, 30, 31

Parenting, 72
Pelvic inflammatory disease (PID), 92

Penis, 16–19
   circumcised or uncircumcised, 16–18
   erection of, 19
   sexual intercourse and, 25
   size of, 19
Petting, 105
Pill, the, 74–75
Pituitary gland, $9n$
Placenta, 33
Pleasure, 5
Pregnancy, 12, 31–41
   drug and alcohol use during, 37–40
   duration of, 32–33
   signs of, 31–32
   teenage, 71–72
   tubal, 90
   without intercourse, 106
Premarital intercourse, 112–13
Premature babies, 36
Prenatal care, 72
Problems of sex, 63–69
Progesterone, 57
Prostate gland, 18–19
Puberty
   in boys, 21, 23
   in girls, 6, 11–12
Pubic hair
   in boys, 21
   in girls, 11

Quickening, 34

Rape, 67–68
Religions, 113. See also Catholic
      Church
Reproduction, 48
Respect for others, 4
Responsibility, 5, 50–51
Rubber (condom), 77–78

Scrotum, 18
Secondary sex characteristics, 57
Selfishness, 63–64, 106–7
Self-respect, 4
Semen, 19–20
Seminal vesicles, 18

Sex. See Sexuality
Sex differences between women and
      men, 52–57
   body differences and, 56
   childrearing and, 54–55
   hormones and, 56–57
Sex roles, 55–56
Sexual arousal, 25
   petting and, 106
Sexual intercourse, 24–27
   animal sex compared to, 48–50
   bad feelings about, 64–65
   first experience with, 26, 27, 108
   incestuous, 66–67
   orgasm during, 25–27
   positions in, 27
   premarital, 112–13
   right time for, 109–11
   saying no to, 107–9
   for selfish needs, 106–7
   slang words for, 68–69
Sexuality, 52–57. See also Bisexuality;
      Homosexuality
   animal and human, 48–51
   decisions about, 100–1
   defined, 52
   expressions of, 54–55
   in men, 53
   similarities between men and women,
      52
   in women, 53–54
Sexually transmitted diseases (STDs),
      88–97, 113
   AIDS, 94
   crabs, 95
   gonorrhea, 89–90
   herpes (genital herpes), 91
   nongonococcal urethritis (NGU), 92
   pelvic inflammatory disease (PID), 92
   prevention, treatment, and cure of,
      95–97
   syphilis, 92–93
   trichomonas (trichomoniasis), 90–91
   urinary infections, 94–95
   yeast infections, 94
Slang words, 68–69
Smoking, during pregnancy, 37